With good wishes

Peter McMam.

RICHTHOFEN
JAGDSTAFFEL AHEAD

By the same author:

One Man's Motorcycles 1939-1949
Boyhood in Rhyl, engineering apprenticeship in Derby,
aero-engine development at Rolls-Royce then starting
in the motorcycle business.

One Man's Scotland
Two centuries and more of Scottish deerstalking together
with the author's 40 year experience.

One Man's Gun Quest
Fifty years search for fine English guns and rifles.

To my grandsons Adam and Clive

RICHTHOFEN JAGDSTAFFEL AHEAD

RFC Pilots Out-Performed and Out-Gunned
over the Western Front, 1917

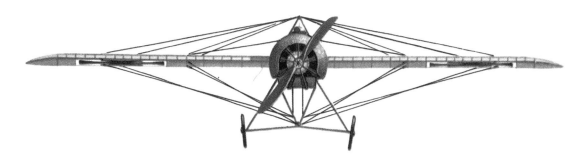

Peter McManus

Grub Street • London

Published by
Grub Street
4 Rainham Close
London
SW11 6SS

British Library Cataloguing in Publication Data
McManus, Peter
Richthofen Jagdstaffel ahead : RFC pilots out-performed and
out-gunned over the Western Front, 1917
1. Blaxland, Lionel 2. Great Britain. Royal Flying Corps
3. Germany. Luftwaffe – History – World War, 1914-1918
4. World War, 1914-1918 – Aerial operations, British
5. World War, 1914-1918 – Aerial operations, German
I. Title II. Batchelor, John H.
940.4'4941

ISBN 978-1-906502-00-3

Cover design by Lizzie B design

The publishers wish to thank Roy Platten (roy.eclipse@btopenworld.com)
for all his hard work on this project.

Printed and bound in Malta

Grub Street Publishing only uses
FSC (Forest Stewardship Council) paper for its books

CONTENTS

The iconic recruiting poster. Lord Kitchener, Secretary of State for War in August 1914 was determined to raise a huge volunteer army.

INTRODUCTION AND ACKNOWLEDGEMENTS

When I was a boy during the nineteen thirties in Rhyl, North Wales, I found World War One aviation a fascinating subject. The new gladiators fighting in single combat through the war-torn skies of the Western Front in France captivated me. I was enthralled by the Biggles stories in the weekly magazine, *The Modern Boy* written by Captain W.E. Johns.

Biggles and his friends flew their Sopwith Camels against the German Albatros and Fokkers. W.E. Johns had, in fact, flown on the Western Front but he flew two-seater bombers, not Sopwith Camels. In his squadron was a Derby man named Wigglesworth, always known as Wiggles, hence when he required a name for his fictional hero he named him Bigglesworth shortened to Biggles.

I knew John Simpkinson of Etwall, Derbyshire who had flown as aircrew in World War Two. He told me that his uncle, Lionel Blaxland, his mother's brother, had flown in 40 Squadron on the Western Front in 1917. One of his fellow pilots was Mick Mannock who went on to become the highest scoring British pilot of the war.

Mannock went to France in early 1917 and joined 40 Squadron as a tyro pilot, yet to encounter the enemy. Lieutenants Blaxland and Lemon were, in fact, to witness Mannock's first victory.

So Lionel Blaxland was a man I had to meet.

At that time he was the vicar of Doveridge, South Derbyshire, not far from Ellastone where my wife Edna and I had a small woodland estate.

Fortunately, I was able to spend time with Lionel Blaxland on a number of occasions and chat to him about those amazing days on the Western Front. So many questions to ask and, luckily, I was able to take lots of notes.

When Lionel died he left his wartime log book which recorded every flight he made in the war on the day. In addition to that he had taken five albums of photographs of the planes and pilots of the time. Strictly speaking such photographs were forbidden but Lionel had taken no notice and snapped away! His photographs have survived against all the odds and have never been published before. These albums, too, were left to John.

All have been very kindly lent to me by him to write the story of Lionel Blaxland, Mick Mannock and his fellow pilots.

Bryan Cooper and John Batchelor are two remarkable men who co-wrote a book called

Fighter some years ago. Bryan is a highly talented historian and writer who owned and edited his own local newspaper while still a teenager! John is an aviation artist of staggering ability whose work, in my opinion, cannot be surpassed. Both these outstanding people have allowed me to use some of their work: Bryan to quote from his text and John to use some of his pictures. All colour illustrations of World War One aircraft are from the John Batchelor Collection. Are the World War One aircraft 20th century sculpture? Of course! Just look at John Batchelor's illustrations.

Computer wizards Dean Bradshaw and Andy MacLeod of Tranters, Derby have put all the photographs on disc, enlarging and enhancing them to achieve results that have astounded me.

Finally I give my unqualified thanks to my wife Edna who has typed out my often unintelligible handwritten manuscript and to Stephanie McManus who has, once again, painstakingly edited the book. She successfully edited my previous trilogy: *One Man's Motorcycles, One Man's Scotland* and *One Man's Gun Quest*. Do not under-estimate the job of editor. It requires a complete command of English, computer literacy, endless time, patience and an eagle eye! In addition to this the whole design and layout of the book is down to Stephanie.

A word on spelling: Albatross is the British spelling, but the German spelling ends with only one 's'. As the Albatros was a German plane the German spelling has been used. When writing the plural of Albatros, rather than using the clumsy Albatroses, I have taken note of Arthur Rhys David's ruling. He was an Etonian and classical scholar who flew in the great SE5a 56 Squadron with Mannock. He always insisted that the correct plural was "Albatri" rather than the "verbal atrocity of Albatroses". It was always used in 56 Squadron and later throughout the RFC. Lionel Blaxland, for example, always referred to "Albatri".

Lieutenant in England is pronounced Leff-tenant but as you well know from American films, Loo-tenant in America though the spelling is the same. The German equivalent is Leutnant i.e. not the same spelling and is pronounced Loitnant (as in Loiter). Some authors use the British equivalent but I have stuck to the German spelling when referring to German ranks.

Unless stated otherwise, photographs are from Lionel Blaxland's personal collection. The captions rely heavily on what he wrote in his albums.

These are Lionel Blaxland's five photograph albums, covering the period 1915 to 1920, together with his flying log book which recorded every flight he made during the war on the day he flew. All lent to Peter McManus to write the story of Lionel Blaxland, Mick Mannock and their fellow pilots.

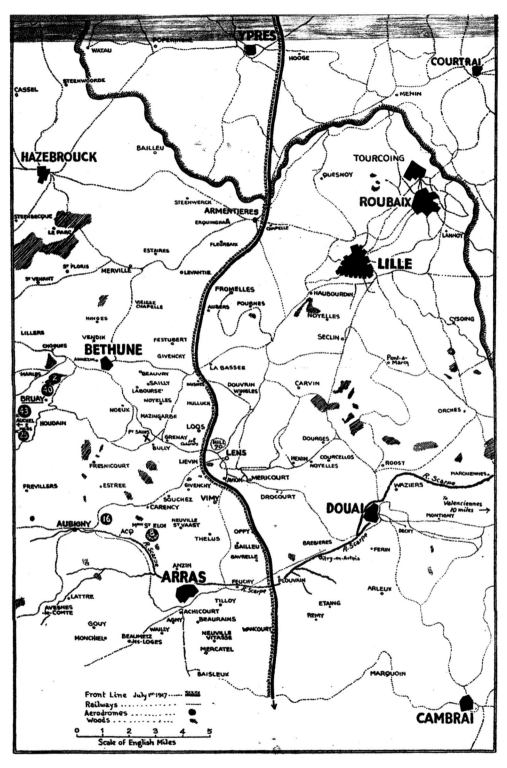

The front line, July 1st 1917 from William MacLanachan's book, *Fighter Pilot*.
McLanachan flew in 40 Squadron with Lionel Bruce Blaxland and Mick Mannock.

Map showing the Alliances in Europe before and during World War One.

1

FRANCE 1917.
THE WESTERN FRONT

March 9th 1917. 8.40 am. Treizennes Airfield not far from Aire on the River Lys and a few miles behind the lines. A bitterly cold March morning. Winter had relentlessly refused to release its grip and the previous two days had meant that flying was impossible but now the primitive pusher FE8s of Number 40 Squadron Royal Flying Corps were lined up on the frosted grass airfield.

Their 100 hp Gnôme rotary engines were lubricated by castor oil, reduced to the consistency of treacle by the low temperature, but they had been heaved into reluctant life, coughing and wheezing, by the sweating mechanics.

The young pilots Neve, Shephard, Hasler, Hills, Maurice, Todd, Cox, Pell and Lionel 'Mac' Blaxland duly climbed into their machines and at 8.45am, throttles opened wide, the machines bumped over the grass and took off for their climb towards the enemy lines.

The FE8 was a strange choice for a single-seater fighter; It was a modification of the two-seater FE2B armed with a forward-firing .303 Lewis gun with a drum containing 97 rounds of ammunition. Once the drum was exhausted there were another two spare drums to be changed…. not so good when the German pilots were shooting at you! It was also found that the Lewis frequently jammed.

The engine and pusher propeller were behind the pilot so he had a clear view… and no protection from the icy blast. Woe betide him if he fumbled and dropped a drum as it could go straight into the propeller. Maximum speed at sea level was about 100mph but much less at 8,000 feet.

At about the same time on the other side of the lines at Brayelle Airfield, Richthofen's Jagdstaffel was preparing for take-off.

Their machines were very different: shark-like Albatros fighters powered by a six-cylinder water-cooled Mercedes engine and armed with twin Spandau belt-fed machine-guns with 1,000 rounds of firepower. So not only had they ten times the firepower of their opponents but they had another great advantage… the Spandaus worked. The Lewis guns didn't for far too much of the time, but more of this later.

The Albatros was 15/20 mph faster than the FE8 and, in addition, had a much superior rate of climb.

The FE8s lumbered up to 8,000 feet and crossed the lines. No sooner had they done so than

Lionel Bruce Blaxland and the highly regarded Padre Keymer. This photograph was taken by Mick Mannock.

Mick Mannock during his early days with 40 Squadron on the Western Front, early 1917. He got off to a slow start, but went on to become the highest-scoring British pilot of the war with 73 victories.

B Flt 40 Squadron FE8s Treizennes. Taken by Lionel Blaxland prior to March 9th 1917. Plane No. 4 is on the left, No. 2 next to it, No. 3 on right. The other number cannot be distinguished.

The deadly Jagdstaffel 11 that faced 40 Squadron about February/March 1917. Richthofen's all red machine is second from the front. (*Imperial War Museum.*)

FE8 flown by 40 Squadron Royal Flying Corps, March 1917. Span 31ft 6 in. Length 23 ft 8 in. Engine 100 hp Gnôme Mono. Armament: One Lewis. Maximum Speed 94 mph ground level. Service ceiling 14,500 ft.

Flown by Richthofen's Jasta, March 11th 1917, this is Leutnant Kurt Wolff's machine, in the colour scheme he adopted later in 1917. Thirty-one victories before being shot down by 10 Squadron Royal Navy Air Service on September 15th 1917. Albatros D3 Span 29 ft 7 in. Length 24 ft. Engine 100 hp Mercedes. Armament: Twin Spandaus. Maximum speed 115 mph. Service ceiling 18,000 ft.

From left to right:
Pell, Brown, Captain
Powell, Henderson,
Hasler.

Two FE8s both numbered 4 safe and sound on their home aerodrome before March 9th 1917.

Wind Direction and Velocity	Machine Type and No.	Passenger	Time	Height	Course	Remarks
	F.E 6426	—	50 min	8000	O.P. Rocker arm broke, five minutes after leaving, patrol attacked by 8 H.A. (circus) Nieve wounded; Shepard, Hassler, Hills missing; Morice, Todd, Cox, Bell, returned with machines shot about very badly.	
	F.E 6426		25 min	2,000	M.G. practice, 3 half drums, 22 hits, 1 bull, broken extractor.	
	F.E. 6426		2hr 11min	8,500	O.P. "Arras" 2 H.A dived through patrol, 3 in distance, no contact with H.A, close. Had Choked jet, engine doing 850 revs; lost 6,000 ft on return, jet cleard near drome, two pieces of falling Archie through left hand plane.	
	New F.E from Omer		15 mins		Fetched new F.E 8 from Omer, (St) very low clouds.	

Photocopy of Lionel Bruce Blaxland's log book for March 9th 1917.

they were met by unusually heavy anti-aircraft fire: *Crrumph, woof*…the planes rocked as they flew past the menacing black, oily bursts of smoke. Always a hair-raising experience but the pilots gritted their teeth and flew on.

Fortunately all got through the barrage safely….this time.

Five minutes after take-off Mac Blaxland's engine started running roughly and the revs dropped. This was later found to be due to a broken rocker arm but he pressed on, trailing behind the rest of the squadron. Eventually he was forced to turn back to endure the anti-aircraft barrage yet again.

Two enemy machines were sighted well into Hunland, but was it a trap? Moments later Manfred von Richthofen led his Jagdstaffel down onto the FE8s.

Richthofen had already scored his twenty-fourth victory by March 9th. He had recently taken command of his first Jasta, Jagdstaffel 11. Although the Jasta had been formed seven months before Richthofen took over it had failed to score a single victory, but Richthofen was determined to change all that.

Despite their lack of success the pilots showed promise: Leutnants Allmenröder, Brockelmann, Esser, Hinch, Hintmann, Mohnicke, Pluchow, Shäfer, Wolff and a number of NCO pilots. Allmenröder, Wolff and Shäfer were to go on and achieve fame under Richthofen's leadership.

Abgeschossen am 9.3.17 bei Annay an der Strasse Lens-Corvin.

Hasler's FE8 driven down 9th March 1917 by the "Circus". The picture was captured in a trench raid near S. Lens.

9/3/17 Shot down by the "Circus". Both pictures are German propaganda postcards.

Richthofen first led his Jasta on January 23rd 1917. At the head of seven Albatros D2s he ran into a flight of 40 Squadron's FE8s. Firing 150 rounds into his victim he shot it down in flames for his seventeenth victory.

On March 9th Richthofen was flying the latest Albatros, a brand new D3. Scenting blood and eager to prove his new machine he selected his victim and opened fire at close range with his twin Spandaus but after only ten rounds had been fired he felt enemy bullets strike his aircraft together with a reduction in engine revs and an overpowering smell of petrol.

Although his machine had been hit, Richthofen himself had not, so desperate action was essential, particularly as his opponent was still shooting at him! Petrol hitting the hot engine or exhaust could transform his plane into a flaming fireball and ominous white petrol mist was already trailing behind.

He switched off the engine and dived steeply but his luck was in and his opponent veered away. He raced earthwards, keeping an anxious lookout behind him when he saw a blazing aeroplane hurtling towards him.

British or German? Fortunately for him he recognised it as British. Moments later another machine spiralled down out of the fight, finally straightening out and flying towards him. It was Shäfer whose machine had also been hit but realising that Richthofen was safe he headed back to the airfield.

Richthofen landed beside the Henin-Liétard road. An officer driving by stopped and gave him a lift to the town only a few kilometres away. Richthofen rang his airfield and was immediately collected by Shäfer, the pilot who had flown down to check on him.

Back at La Brayelle Richthofen was in the air again only about an hour from having landed, hoping to cut off the FE8s on their way home. He was unable to do this but over Roclincourt, just north of Arras, he encountered a DH2 pusher fighter and shot it down in flames, killing the pilot 2nd Lt. Arthur J. Pearson MC for his twenty-fifth victory.

Having been forced to turn back due to that broken rocker arm Mac Blaxland's plane was undamaged but he recorded in his log book: "Neve wounded. Shephard, Hasler, Hills missing, Maurice, Todd, Cox, Pell, returned with machines shot about very badly."

Shephard was shot down by Lt. Kurt Wolff and his machine landed upside down but he survived and was taken prisoner.

2

INTRODUCING LIONEL BRUCE BLAXLAND 1898-1976

The inclusion of 'Bruce' in the family name denoted the Blaxland's Scottish ancestry. John Simpkinson's mother, for example, was Miss Athol Bruce Blaxland. Athol is a most unusual girl's name but she was a most unusual girl! She rode a motorcycle and drove a Crossley tender in the Royal Flying Corps in World War One.

The Blaxlands all fought in World War One. Eldest brother Jack, was killed at Kut in what is now Iraq. People are still being killed there today!

Second brother Alan Bruce Blaxland, born in 1893, fought in two world wars: Sherwood Foresters 1914-1918, Indian Army between the wars then OC in Cyprus for most of World War Two retiring with the rank of lieutenant general. Their father was Vicar of the Abbey Church, Shrewsbury and our man Lionel was educated at Shrewsbury School.

Haughton Hill 1915.
M MacLeod, CBB, LBB, N MacLeod

ABB, CBB, MM

The above are LBB's captions. LBB is, of course, Lionel Bruce Blaxland, CBB is sister Constance, ABB is sister Athol. The MacLeods were, presumably, family friends.

MM, P Puckle, CBB, NM, LBB 1915   *P Puckle, CBB, MM, ABB, N Mac, 1915*

The Home Front. Carefree days with motorcycles and a family picnic.

After the war he gained a history degree at Oriel College, Oxford, and started as a master at Repton Public School in 1922. He became a housemaster at The Hall. The other sister Constance Bruce Blaxland nursed in World War One and married Leonard Catley, MC. During the Second World War he became housemaster of Priory House, Repton. Athol's husband (John Simpkinson's father) died in 1943 and she went on to live with her sister Constance and brother-in-law, Leonard, at the Priory. Cross House had been closed during the war but re-opened in 1945 with Lionel as housemaster. Athol joined him to help. They remained there until retirement in 1958.

He then spent a year visiting relatives in Australia and finally, surprisingly, joined the church becoming the Vicar of Doveridge, Derbyshire, which is when I met him.

Strangely enough all John Simpkinson's three sisters married men with Repton connections. Two were Reptonians and the third lived in Repton though was educated at Oundle.

Lionel eventually retired to Bridge near Canterbury. Always a sportsman he had gained a soccer Blue and played for the Corinthians in the FA Cup. The Corinthians at that time were considered to be the most successful amateur team and competed against professional teams, the last amateur team to do so. On one occasion they beat Aston Villa. Later, he played cricket for Derbyshire in the 1930s and just after the war in 1946/47 he captained Derbyshire against Alan Melville's South Africans.

John Simpkinson tells me that Lionel was a marvellous uncle and always great fun to be with. He had a tremendous zest for life, tackling everything with enormous enthusiasm. He was an enthusiastic teacher with the ability to transfer that enthusiasm to his pupils. No, he never did get married but according to John he did have two close encounters!

Top: The two attractive sisters, Athol and Constance with their lives ahead of them in 1916.

Above and right: The Abbey Vicarage – the family home in Shrewsbury.

Shrewsbury 1916 – P Miles, HRP Ward, LBB, CR Harman, unknown.

9/3/17 – This is Lionel enjoying some off-duty time but surely the date in his album cannot be correct as this is the date of 40 Squadron's epic encounter with Richthofen's Jasta 11.

1915 – Athol Bruce Blaxland (left) warmly dressed for motoring. Just look at those gloves! The car could be an RFC Crossley. Brother Alan is above right.

Athol on Douglas (Nadier's) 1916.   *3 miles from Wem, going.*

The above are Lionel's captions remarking on Athol Bruce Blaxland experiencing the joys of motorcycling. Note the butt-ended inner tube for easy roadside repair. The bike on the left was a 350 side-valve Douglas twin. Two speed, no kick start.

3

LIONEL BLAXLAND AND NO. 40 SQUADRON 1917

Lionel Bruce Blaxland was one of the early breed of air fighters, pioneers who fought in the skies over the Western Front in 1914-1918. Air fighting was in its infancy and initially Lionel and his colleagues in 40 Squadron in 1914-1918 flew the pusher FE8 'fighters' against the deadly and far more advanced Albatros D2s and D3s. With the welcome change to the nimble Nieuport 17s in late March 1917 the chances of survival were greatly improved but the armament was still a single Lewis gun mounted on the top plane and firing over the propeller. In addition, the gun had to be hauled down and a new drum clipped on after 97 rounds had been fired. Lionel explained to me how exhausting this operation was at high altitude.

This was a momentous period in the air war and included 'Bloody April' when British aviation losses rocketed to a new high. So to understand this it is important to look at the way it all came about. Here is a brief account.

War in the air was entirely new in 1914. The first man to fly the English Channel was Louis Blériot only six years before. The war had quickly settled into stalemate with the armies facing each other in trench systems that stretched from the Channel coast to Switzerland.

Before 1914 the cavalry units were the eyes of the army but there was no chance of deploying cavalry over the churned up waste of no-man's-land and its barbed wire entanglements, so the new air arm took over the cavalry's role.

Reconnaisance was vital for both sides to observe their opponents so fighter aircraft evolved, again on both sides, to shoot down the enemy's two-seater reconnaissance planes.

Initially the Germans attached two or three fighters to each reconnaissance unit. The British and French, however, formed complete fighter units and the Royal Flying Corps commander, Major General Hugh Trenchard, firmly believed in taking the fight to the enemy with unrelenting offensive tactics.

The Germans, however, adopted a more defensive role letting the British, French and Belgian aircraft come to them. The prevailing westerly winds favoured the Germans, pushing the opposing aircraft over their territory and making it difficult for them to fight against the wind to fly back.

In any event the German air power was inferior to the combined numbers available to the Allies.

However, the fortunes of the air war swung like a pendulum throughout the war years.

Gurney, Hall, Sergeant Bone, Sergeant Mather. No. 1 C Flight.

One side would achieve superiority, then the other. The Germans seized the upper hand during the period August 1915 to June 1916 with the Fokker Eindekker (monoplane) with its forward-firing machine-gun synchronised to fire through the propeller. This period became known as the 'Fokker Scourge'.

The Eindekker was a deadly machine in the hands of Immelmann, Boelcke and their fellow pilots. But the Fokker Scourge was finally curbed after Boelcke's death for a number of reasons during the late autumn of 1916. We now tend to look back on the pusher British aircraft as antiquated monstrosities and the term 'pusher fighter' as an oxymoron but this is far too simplistic a view. The pushers did have a role to play in aviation history and they did help to curb the Fokker Scourge.

The Eindekker could fly towards its enemy and open fire because of its formidable Spandau. The British pushers could do the same so could, at last, face the Eindekker on something like equal terms though, of course, with far inferior firepower.
The single-seater pusher fighter DH2, despite being bitterly cold to fly, effectively checked the Eindekker. The similar FE8s were only issued to two squadrons so they had little impact.

But the two-seater 'pusher fighters' could also fire forward and were used effectively. For example, the FE2Bs. Better British aircraft were not to be available until May 1917 but halting the Eindekker's dominance was not merely due to the opposition of the pushers.

This is where Trenchard's policy of all-out offensive paid off though, of course, at great cost in aircrew casualties. The RFC was far more aggressive than the German flying services, taking the initiative by flying across the lines into enemy territory. The Germans, as previously explained, tended to keep in their own air space.

So with the Eindekkers having faced formidable opposition did the balance of power then decisively swing in the Allies' favour? No, it didn't. Worse was to come.

Before the end of 1916 a new breed of German fighter had arrived at the front. Halberstadt D2s and Albatros D2s, biplane fighters that out-performed their opponents and had superior firepower too. Both were armed with twin Spandaus with a total of 1,000 rounds capacity.

Boelcke was not only a formidable fighter but he had the vision to create fighting squadrons known as Jagstaffeln or Jastas. This brilliant concept took off with seven squadrons in October 1916 and by early spring 1917, thirty-seven had been formed.

These Jagstaffeln were given a tremendous boost by the new biplane fighters, so the DH2 and FE8 pushers, the FE2B pushers and the Sopwith 1^1/$_2$ Strutters, Sopwith Pups and Nieuport 17s were all outclassed.

Despite the Somme disaster of 1916 the Allies, with endless optimism, had planned another big push for spring 1917 and although Field Marshal Haig had pressed the War Cabinet for better aircraft, none could be available in time.

But just why were the German fighter pilots so successful in the first half of 1917? First of all, of course, their aircraft were superior in performance and firepower.

Secondly, for most of the time, they were able to wait for opponents to come to them by crossing into their own territories so they did not have to face enemy AA fire. When they brought a machine down it was over their own land so confirmation of victories was not in doubt.

When they broke off combat, unlike their opponents, they did not have to fight against the prevailing winds to get back home.

Another important factor was pilot training. Trenchard's policy of rushing out poorly trained pilots who were so easily shot down did not apply to the Germans. German pilots were usually promoted to fly fighters after having first flown two-seaters, so they already had the experience of combat which gave them an enormous advantage.

Machines on advanced landing ground.

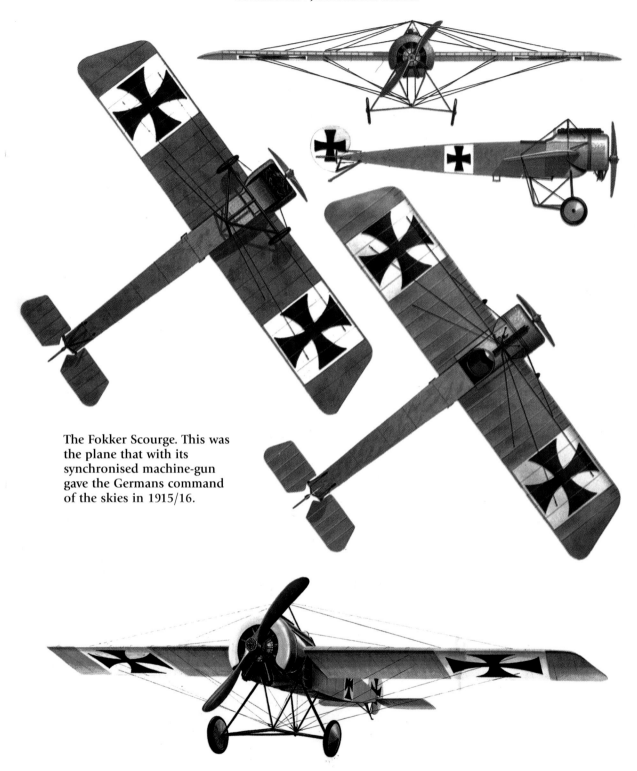

The Fokker Scourge. This was the plane that with its synchronised machine-gun gave the Germans command of the skies in 1915/16.

The Fokker Eindekker E3. Span 32 ft 6 in. Length 23 ft 6 in. Engine 110 hp Oberursel. Armament: Twin Spandaus (though the earlier marques had a single Spandau). Maximum speed: 87 mph. Maximum service ceiling 12,000 ft.

4

LEARNING TO FLY

On August 28th 1916, Lionel, aged 18, joined the Royal Flying Corps at Oxford for preliminary instruction. The RFC cadets were housed in the various colleges with instruction being given in wooden buildings on the perimeter of Port Meadow. He passed the examination on October 7th and after a short leave joined the Central Flying School at Upavon commencing flying training as a pupil on a Maurice Farman Shorthorn on October 20th.

He left Upavon on November 11th and was posted to D Squadron at the Central Flying School, Netheravon. He then flew as a pupil on Henri Farmans, graduating to a Vickers Gun-Bus, next to a De Haviland Scout, a pusher single-seater and finally to an FE8, single-seater pusher fighter that he was destined to fly in earnest on the Western Front.

He got his wings on 26th December 1916 after 27 hours 45 minutes flying and reported for overseas duty at Adastral House, London on January 29th 1917.

Those Maurice Farman 'Shorthorns' and Henri Farmans look unbelievably flimsy to us today with the aerodynamic qualities of a combine harvester but without the solidity. It must be remembered, however, that they were very early designs when so little was known about aviation.

Henri Farman started building aeroplanes in 1908 and, believe it or not, his 1909 pusher was considered to be such a good aeroplane that it was copied by others. His brother, Maurice, was also an aeroplane designer and in 1912 Henri, Maurice and their brother Dick joined forces to build aeroplanes. Henri and Maurice, however, still designed independently so the nomenclature Henri Farman and Maurice Farman continued. Realising that war was inevitable they expanded their factory and on the outbreak of war they were the only factory capable of accepting large orders.

The Henri Farman F20s, F21s and F22s of 1913 were already in service with the British, French and Belgian services by the time that war was declared, powered by 70 or 80 hp Gnôme or 80 hp Le Rhône rotaries. Clearly they were underpowered and only suitable for training or undemanding reconnaissance and by the summer of 1915 they were relegated to training.

The Maurice Farman MF7s of 1913 were powered by Renault engines of between 70 and 100 hp or 100 hp Lorraines. The Type 1914 or MF11s (called the Shorthorn by the British) were powered by various engines: Renaults and De Dions of 70-130 hp and even Curtiss and 75 hp Rolls-Royce Hawks. They were flown by many French escadrilles and a number of British

Maurice Farman MF11 Shorthorn. Span 53 ft, length 31 ft. Engine 100 hp De Dion. Maximum speed 93 mph.

Maurice Farman (S.H.) 80 Renault. Netheravon 1916 (Oct). LBB's first solo after 3 hours, 20 minutes.

squadrons, too, flew them on the Western Front. By late 1915, however, they were replaced in British Squadrons by BE2Cs though they continued in use for training throughout the war. Performance: Henri Farman F20 about 65mph. Maurice Farman MF11 Shorthorn about 70mph.

Flying the Shorthorn was a strange experience: with a maximum speed of 60-70mph it was no scalded cat! The simple dashboard only contained a compass, air speed indicator, altimeter and side-slip bubble plus a temperature gauge if fitted with a water-cooled engine.

Unreliability and even engine failure were constant hazards and, in addition, the Le Rhône rotaries were very prone to choking i.e. an over-rich mixture causing the engine to falter or fail. Forced landings were inevitable.

Vickers FB 26. This was a development of the FB12 and the end of the line for pushers.

Leading Aircraftman William Roberts died, aged 105, on April 30th 2006. He joined the RFC as a fitter and rigger aged 17. His service career was entirely in England and he started flying as a passenger as this was considered easier than carrying ballast.

His first flight was on a Maurice Farman pusher which turned over on take-off. The Belgian pilot dragged him clear of the wreckage in case it caught fire. An hour later the same pilot took off again on another machine but this time the plane crashed and killed him.

In later life William Roberts was haunted by the tragic losses of "many good young men" who were killed in training whilst flying aircraft that were "not very good"!

All pilots remember the excitement…and apprehension…of their early training and Lionel was no exception. His first flight was with instructor Lt. Ryan on October 21st 1916. He wrote in his log book "First time up. Felt very dizzy at first but then liked it very much".

First training flights were round the aerodrome, short flights at between 500 and 1,000 feet, practicing take-offs, landings and simple manoeuvres. Early in the day and early evening were considered to be ideal times for novices to fly as, for some unaccountable reason, wind speeds seemed at their lowest at 5am and 5pm.

"The air's bumpy today," the instructor would solemnly declare or "There's no lift in the air today".

Lectures were attended on the theory of flight, aero engines, navigation, meteorology etc. by the trainee pilots, anxious to get out of the classroom and into the air and as they gained confidence and experience, cross-country flights were made.

Memorable moments for Lionel were the first time he took over the controls, the wobbly take-offs and landings, first solo flight, first heart-stopping forced landing, first cross-country flight, first flight in a real fighter and the enormous triumph of being awarded those coveted wings. In spite of many hair-raising moments, Lionel never had a bad crash during his training.

Lionel then graduated to a two-seater fighter, the Vickers FB5 Gun-Bus. The Vickers company were sure that war was inevitable and had experimented with pusher machines fitted

FB5 (Vickers) Span 36 ft 6 in, length 27 ft 2 in Engine 100 hp Gnôme Mono. Armament: one Lewis. Maximum speed 70 mph at 5,000 ft. Service ceiling 9,000 ft.

DH2. Span 28 ft 3 in. Length 25 ft 2 in, Engine 100 hp Gnôme Mono. Armament: one Lewis. Maximum speed 93 mph at ground level. Service ceiling 14,000 ft.

with a machine-gun. The culmination was the Vickers FB5 two-seater fighter so they took a chance and built 50 of them without having received a government order. These 'fighters' arrived in France in February 1915 and one or two were attached to units to provide protection for reconnaissance machines. They were fitted with the 100 hp Monosoupé rotary engine and speed was about 75mph.

In July 1915 the FB5s formed the first two-seater fighter squadron to be sent to France and initially they were quite successful but by November 1915 they were outclassed by the deadly Fokker Eindekkers.

The FB5s were updated to FB9s in December 1915 but it appears that they were only used in training units.

The next step for Lionel was a single-seater fighter, the DH2. This was the second type designed by Geoffrey de Havilland: a pusher because it was designed to carry a forward-firing

Not a remarkable photograph but a rare front view of an FE8 in Lionel's album.

machine-gun and at that time no British interrupter gear enabling a machine-gun to fire through the propeller was available. Racks for spare Lewis gun drums were on either side of the cockpit.

The first single-seater fighter squadron, No. 24, went to France with DH2s in February 1916, commanded by Major L.G. Hawker, VC. It helped to combat the deadly Fokker Eindekkers. The DH2s were powered by either the 100hp Monosoupé or 110 hp Le Rhône rotaries with a speed of about 90mph.

By the autumn of 1916 the new German Albatros D types and Halberstadts armed with twin Spandaus firing through the propeller had arrived and they made mincemeat of the DH2s, but they had to soldier on into the summer when modern replacements started to come on stream.

Like all the pushers they were bitterly cold machines to fly. Jimmy McCudden flew DH2s through the winter of 1916/17 and wrote after a patrol: "I did not care whether I was shot down or not; I was so utterly frozen."

FE8 'crashed'. An all too common fate.

Towards the end of his training Lionel mostly flew DH2s but he did manage one hour and twenty-five minutes on an FE8, the machines he would fly in France with 40 Squadron.

The FE8 was very like the DH2 and designed as a pusher for the same reason, i.e to enable a forward-firing machine-gun to be fitted. It was designed by J. Kenworthy of the Royal Aircraft Factory and powered by the Monosoupé rotary.

Both the DH2 and the FE8 were prone to spinning and pilots were killed before Major Gooden, the factory test pilot, demonstrated how to get the machines out of a spin.

Racks for spare Lewis gun drums were fitted on either side of the nacelle. Performance and speed were about the same as the DH2.

Production delays meant that the first to reach France were with 40 Squadron in August 1916 and a second squadron, 41, was equipped with them in October. The FE8 was, like the DH2, completely outclassed by the Albatri and Halberstadts right from the start. Only 300 were built and, fortunately, no other squadrons were equipped with them.

5

ARRIVAL IN FRANCE

On January 31st 1917 Lionel crossed the Channel and arrived at Treizennes Airfield with 40 Squadron RFC in the British Expeditionary Force on February 2nd.

Lionel explained to me that the most overwhelming asset of flying in World War One was the tremendous camaraderie. There were only a few pilots in a squadron and it was like being in an extended family with, "One for all and all for one".

In addition to that was Padre Keymer who was attached to No. 40 and adjoining squadrons. Lionel told me that he was regarded with great affection by everyone in the squadrons. He was "guide, philosopher and friend" to them all.

Keymer was greatly affected by the deaths of the pilots to whom he had been so closely attached. He was, said Lionel, "always supportive and completely un-stuffy. We were all," he said, "very fortunate to have him and very much in his debt."

Lionel told me how Mannock used to love to engage the padre in tongue-in-cheek arguments with the intention of making him loose his cool....but he never did. They were always answered with tolerance and humour.

The CO was the colourful character, Robert Loraine. Robert was a famous actor before and after the war and a very early pilot. He had attempted to be the first man to fly over the Irish Sea before the war in an Antoinette and *almost* made it.

February 3rd, 4th, and 5th were taken up with practice flying and machine-gun practice behind the lines until on February 6th Lionel flew over the lines for the first time experiencing the devilish danger of anti-aircraft fire.

During four flights on the 7th and on the 8th his flight was attacked by eight enemy aircraft. Richthofen himself was at home in Schweidnitz for a short leave but Jasta 11 aircraft were still in action. Lionel escaped with a bullet through his rudder. Beginners luck!

Two flights were made on 10th February and this time attacked by four enemy aircraft and Lionel claimed one 'probable'. He got into a bad spin that took him down from 7,000 feet to 4,000 feet but managed to straighten out.

Captain Keymer in BE2E.

The padre Captain Keymer 40 Squadron.

L's FE8 (100 Mono) fitted
with camera gun.

Captain Powell.

Captain Rosewall Gregory.

SA Short.

From left to right: Cox, Powell, Mulholland, Smith, Hesler.

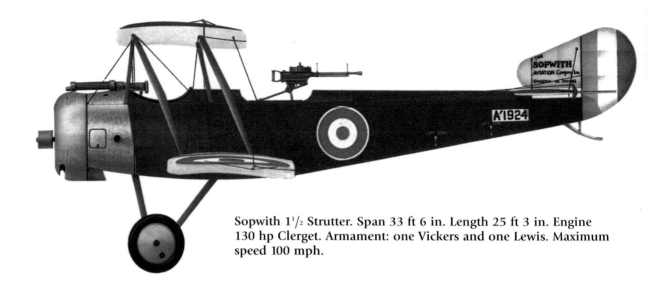

Sopwith 1$\frac{1}{2}$ Strutter. Span 33 ft 6 in. Length 25 ft 3 in. Engine 130 hp Clerget. Armament: one Vickers and one Lewis. Maximum speed 100 mph.

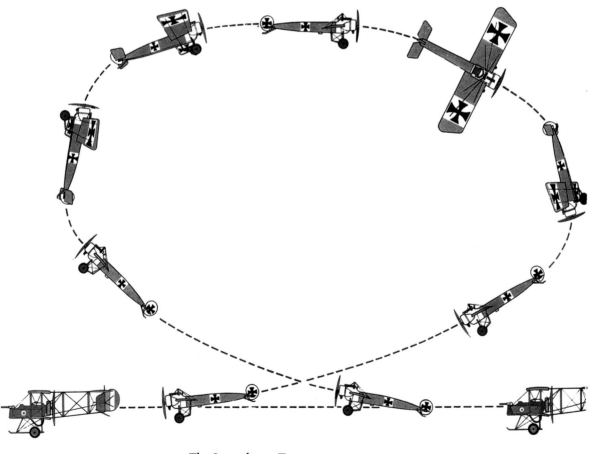

The Immelman Turn.

6

NO. 43 SQUADRON

Sharing the airfield at Treizennes was 43 Squadron, whose commanding officer was the young Sholto Douglas, who was to make his mark in two world wars. In the Second World War he become commander-in-chief of Fighter Command where his First World War experience was to be of vital assistance. Lionel and his fellow pilots knew all the 43 pilots.

43 Squadron flew Sopwith $1^1/_2$ Strutters. Two-seaters designed to be a match for the German fighters but that was early in 1916 and they did have the advantage of a synchronised forward-firing Vickers gun and the observer had a Lewis. By late 1916, however, the Germans had their new Albatros fighters which were a very different proposition.

The $1^1/_2$ Strutter was already out-dated by the time 43 Squadron arrived with them at Treizennes in January 1917. They were much slower than the new Albatros and Halberstadt fighters ranged against them. The more powerful six-cylinder water-cooled engine gave far better all round performance in speed and rate of climb. In addition to that their performance at high altitudes was far in advance of the $1^1/_2$ Strutters whose rotary engine's performance deteriorated rapidly above 10,000 feet.

The $1^1/_2$ Strutters were also none too rugged and with clumsy handling they could, and did, break up in the air.

Once 43 Squadron had started flying against the enemy at Treizennes their losses were far heavier than had been anticipated. This necessitated a constant flow of replacement aircraft, pilots and observers.

The voracious demand for new pilots meant that they were rushed over from England insufficiently trained so Sholto Douglas took it upon himself to give a great deal of instruction to the tyro pilots.

The spring of 1917 was the worst period of the war, up to then, for aircraft and aircrew casualties. Grimly named 'Bloody April', though March had been bad enough when the RFC lost 125 aircraft with 55 shot down in the British lines and 61 in the German lines.

In April 43 Squadron suffered over 100% losses! Not that all the aircrews were shot down, though only six or seven of them survived. The problem was that the rookie replacements were all too often quickly shot down, more often than not within a few days. The squadron was composed of 32 pilots and observers but by the end of the month they had suffered 35 casualties.

GB Crole.

'Boom' Trenchard, the general officer commanding the RFC in France, was warmly regarded by the pilots under his command. Not the most articulate of men but, nonetheless, his humanity shone through. He was, without doubt, very worried about the dreadful aircrew losses but his policy of unrelenting attack was the inevitable result.

Trenchard also knew, as early as the start of 1916, that pilots being sent to France were not properly trained and this knowledge did, indeed, lead to better training. Better it may well have been, but it was still far from good enough.

As noted earlier, Trenchard was determined to pursue a relentless attack on the enemy so inevitably new pilots and new squadrons were rushed out regardless. Sholto Douglas's loyalty to Trenchard never wavered but he was not alone in squadron commanders who believed that Trenchard was mistaken in his policy.

Sholto wrote, "I have always felt that we would have been much better off if we had fewer squadrons manned by pilots who were better trained and who had better experience."

Sholto also believed that Trenchard was wrong in his belief that bombers did not need fighter escorts. This meant that the bombers suffered severe casualties when attacked by Jagdstaffeln of enemy fighters with their superior performance and armament.

So the lesson had to be learnt the hard way by the unfortunate aircrew out there at the sharp end. But, strangely enough, the lesson had to be re-learned during the Second World War. By 1942 the American heavy bombers with vastly superior performance than their World War One predecessors were thought, by the top brass, to be perfectly capable of seeing off the German Messerschmitt 109s. But, once again, it was not to be and after unacceptable losses all American daylight bombers were finally accompanied by long-range fighters.

One of Sholto's pilots was Harold Balfour, aged 20 and already a captain. Tall, slim, and alert he was well above average intelligence. He had already seen a great deal of active service on the ground with the army and in the air with 60 Squadron. His tremendous personality personified the spirit of the Royal Flying Corps. After the war he wrote *An Airman Marches*, a valuable account of his war years. During the Second World War he was Secretary of State for Air. Balfour described their offensive patrols to protect artillery observation aircraft. Even as they crossed the lines they could see the German fighters ahead, waiting for them.

Lionel Bruce Blaxland.

"From afar," he wrote, "we could watch these gaily painted Albatros' gambolling around each other. They would be over Lens, looping, rolling and spinning, just like puppies with each other; but directly we got over our objective away they would swoop into the sun only to wait for the propitious moment in which to come headlong down on the top of our formation."

Sholto found, from experience, that the way to cope with these attacks was for the flight to go into a tight circle with each aircraft on the tail of the one in front, rather like the wagon trains under Indian attack in the Old West. Still in the circle they would then edge their way back over the lines. When the German fighters stooped onto the formation they would be met by the withering fire from all the observers but woe-betide any $1^1/_2$ Strutter that fell out of the circle because it would face certain death.

What a frustrating way to mount an 'Offensive Patrol'.

Sometimes 40 Squadron's FE8s accompanied 43's $1^1/_2$ Strutters as fighter escorts but, Lionel Blaxland told me, that in this case the $1^1/_2$ Strutters had to throttle back to allow the FE8 fighters to keep up with them.

Another staunch colleague of Sholto's was Jock Scott, widely admired throughout and a successful barrister before the war who had, unusually, become a pilot and was an experienced flyer. He had been associated with the great advocate Lord Birkenhead and was a friend of Winston Churchill.

Always something of a clumsy pilot he had broken both legs early in the war and could only walk with two sticks. He had to be lifted in and out of his aircraft.

When 43 Squadron was being formed at Stirling the depot of the Argyll and Sutherland Highlanders was based at Stirling Castle. Their adjutant was Tom Purdey, a member of the great gunsmiths family. He wangled a transfer to the RFC and Sholto Douglas had him appointed to 43 Squadron as recording officer.

Tom Purdey was a cheerful, outgoing character who became enormously popular. He was 'non-flying' of course, and like Padre Keymer, he too gave invaluable support to the squadron.

LBB's machine No. 1. C Flt. George Mather, A M Bone.

From Left to right: Gurney, Hall, Sergeant Mather. No. 1. C Flt.

7

BLOODY APRIL

The arrival of spring and better weather gave the German Jastas the opportunity they had been waiting for. It was one that they grabbed enthusiastically. They had become more aggressive with their new aircraft and it was clear to Trenchard that they would prove to be a formidable obstacle that the RFC would find difficult or even impossible to surmount. His answer was to ask his pilots to fly even more aggressively to defeat the enemy, as although the enemy was superior in ability, they were fewer in numbers. But how could minnows fight pike?

Trenchard also knew that another big offensive was planned for the spring so British reconnaissance would be of vital importance.

The plan was for a massive offensive along a 100-mile front between Arras in the north and the river Aisne in the south. Field Marshal Sir Douglas Haig would command the British and General Robert Nivelle, hero of Verdun in 1916, would command the French.

Trenchard had warned General Haig that newer, more efficient aircraft were essential and Haig had pressed the War Cabinet to supply them but, of course, they could not be produced overnight.

Even before April the latest Albatros, the D3, had started to be issued to the Jastas. Some RNAS squadrons had Sopwith Pups and Triplanes and the French Spad VII was slowly becoming available though only two British squadrons had them, so although the Fokker Scourge had been endured and eventually mastered, much worse lay ahead.

Winter weather had reduced flying by both sides but the casualty figures told a story: in October and November 1916 aircraft casualties did not exceed double figures but in March 1917 British patrols increased to 14,500 and casualties to 143.

When the Arras offensive commenced, the British Army bore the brunt of the fighting and the RFC had 25 squadrons along the length of the front with 365 operational machines, a third of which were fighters. Other squadrons faced the northern section between Lille and Ypres.

The German 6 Army commanded the area Lille in the north to Cambrai in the south with 195 operational aircraft half of which were fighters. But of course, although inferior in numbers they were way ahead in efficiency.

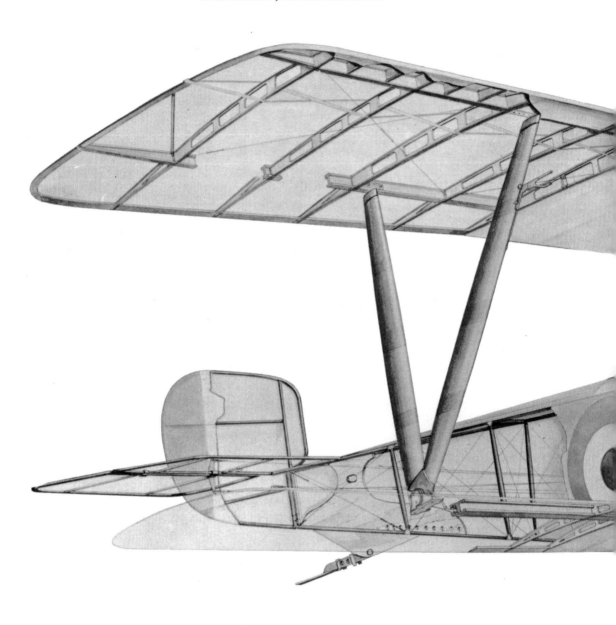

Nieuport 17. Span 26 ft 10 in. Length 18 ft 11 in.
Engine 110 hp Le Rhône. Armament: Lewis gun on
top plane. Maximum speed 107 mph at 6,500 ft.
Service ceiling 17,400 (though in reality, far higher).

Left: GB Crole. Later taken prisoner when flight commander (Camel) Squadron (left wing $^3/_4$ for Scotland and Oxon). Later Indian Civil Service.

Right: Barlow, GB Crole (Barlow killed due to wings coming off Nieuport when rolling.)

Left: Lt. Hall (South Africa). Later on night fighters (Camel) in England. Back to South Africa after the war.

Right: 190 hp Mercedes from Albatros Scout shot down in flames near Arras.

Flight Sergeant Hancock, Sergeants Jackson and Fletcher, Hill. Mannock in machine.

Major Tilney arriving advanced landing ground on Sopwith Pup.

Nieuport Scout. This is Major Tilney, CO of 40 Squadron.

Look at the angle of his Nieuport's Lewis gun, clearly not in line with the line of flight. The factory supplied the aircraft with their machine-guns set at an angle of 15° to the line of flight.

FE2D 250 hp Rolls-Royce.

8

THE BATTLE OF ARRAS

When, at the Calais Conference in February 1917 Generals Douglas Haig and William Robertson were told that they were to be under French command, they both seriously considered resigning. This led Lloyd George to change his mind but Haig was forced to accept a plan with which he disagreed. He wanted to start an offensive in the north to free the Channel ports as those in German hands were being used to enhance their deadly U-boat campaign. The French, however, had a different view. They had planned a massive offensive at Verdun, further south. Haig's part was to support the French by launching an attack some 14 miles long opposite the British lines north and south of Arras. This was some 25 miles south-east of Treizennes Airfield so both 40 and 43 Squadrons were to be involved.

The offensive was launched on Easter Monday April 9th. Winter still held the land in its relentless grip and flying was hampered by south-westerly squalls with rain, sleet and even snow to make flying difficult.

The terrain was dominated by Vimy Ridge, about three miles north of Arras and held by the Germans.

On the afternoon of the first day Sholto took off with another aircraft as No. 43's role was to reconnoitre and photograph.

Over the lines near Arras they spotted an enemy two-seater well above them and gave chase. Several miles later thunderous AA fire opened up and Sholto's engine was hit. The engine started to falter so Sholto had to turn back and hoped to be able to cross the lines, losing height all the time.

He was able to get over the lines with very little height to spare but unable to reach his airfield, he was forced to land on a piece of devastated ground covered with the remains of a disused trench system. He did manage to put the machine down on a small open space with the propeller hanging over an old trench. Fortunately, neither Sholto nor his observer were hurt and the plane was dismantled and returned to Treizennes by road.

Harold Balfour, later in the battle, also suffered a similar fate. He was flying over the German lines with the prevailing westerly wind pushing him further east and heavily subjected to ground fire, until eventually his engine was hit.

He just managed to clear Vimy Ridge and then crashed into the edge of a mine crater. Despite the danger of AA fire he had omitted to strap himself in but on this occasion it saved his life. He was thrown out of the plane just before the engine slammed back into the pilot's seat; as it was he landed head first into the mud. Canadian soldiers rushed out from a dugout, dragging Balfour and his injured observer to safety. The Germans then destroyed the aeroplane by shellfire.

Balfour suffered concussion and was severely stressed as the disaster followed the exhausting and, indeed, terrifying flying he had had to endure. He was "crying to myself with fright and self pity".

Sholto Douglas wrote, "it was a state that any man who makes a claim to honesty would be only too ready to acknowledge."

For the British the Battle of Arras started with a degree of success but for the Royal Flying Corps the dreadful weather badly hampered air reconnaissance. This prevented efficient spotting of German reserves and, as usual, the battle on the ground came to a standstill in a couple of days.

A week later the French General Nivelle launched his attack. He had prophesised that it would be "a day of glory for France". He was wrong. It was a shocking failure.

The Germans held documents revealing the plans for the attack and in addition to this, before the attack, between four and five hundred French pilots had been sent to Le Bourget to collect new aircraft but their instructions were vague and Gay Paree called! The result was that many of them failed to return until the second day of the attack.

The French were badly beaten, disillusion set in and rumours of a revolution in Russia together with mysterious rumours of General Marchington's resignation resulted in a series of mutinies at the front and disloyalty at home.

These mutinies struck at the heart of the French army. The Germans knew something of them but not the full extent. Had they done so and acted immediately and decisively the war could have been won for them.

FB12. The end of the pusher era. Span 26 ft. Length 21 ft 6 in. Engine 100 hp Gnôme Mono. Armament: one Lewis. Maximum speed 93 mph at 5,000 ft. Service ceiling 14,000 ft.

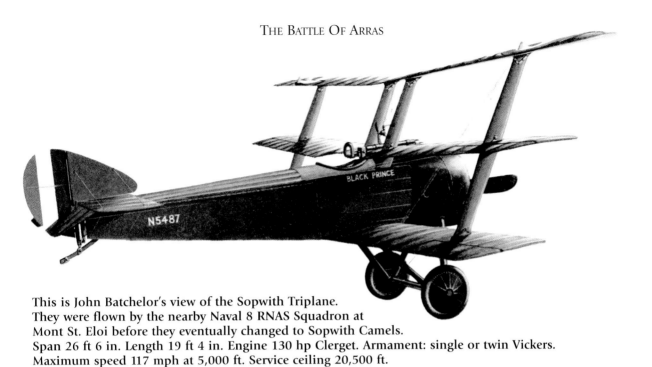

This is John Batchelor's view of the Sopwith Triplane.
They were flown by the nearby Naval 8 RNAS Squadron at
Mont St. Eloi before they eventually changed to Sopwith Camels.
Span 26 ft 6 in. Length 19 ft 4 in. Engine 130 hp Clerget. Armament: single or twin Vickers.
Maximum speed 117 mph at 5,000 ft. Service ceiling 20,500 ft.

The plane illustrated is one of the highly sucessful Black Flight No.10 RNAS with all-Canadian pilots.

BE2C. Mannock and Barlow. The two-seater BE2Cs and Es were inherently stable aeroplanes and first
appeared in France in late 1914, powered by the 90 and 100 hp RAF engines. Speed at ground level
was only 90 mph and ceiling appeared to be about 10,000 feet but they did see service on the
Western Front.

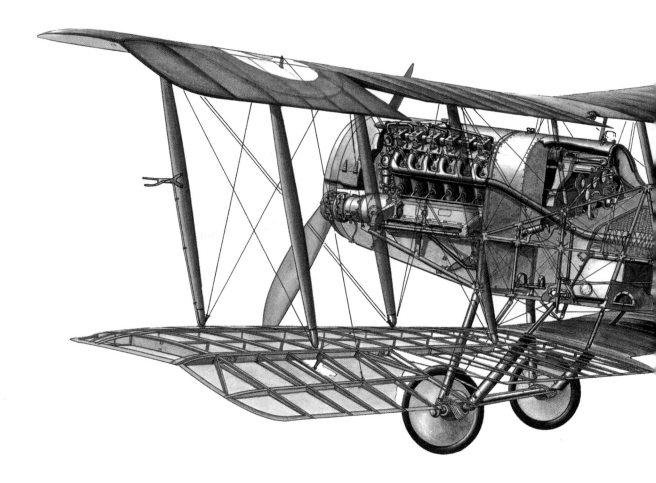

This setback for the French meant that Haig had to keep up the pressure on the British Front for far longer than he had planned so the RFC were forced to work ever more strenuously. Losses mounted and in the space of a mere five days the RFC lost 75 aircraft, 105 pilots and observers with 19 killed, 13 wounded and 73 missing.

There were many more flying accidents, too, with 56 planes written off. Even the official historian later admitted that these heavy losses by accidents were due in part to inefficiency of training which had been speeded up to the danger point.

As previously explained, this lack of training had long worried Sholto Douglas and the results were as he had predicted. These were momentous days and in the same week America entered the war against Germany.

On April 5th the new two-seater Bristol Fighter made its first appearance on the front. This was a rugged, attractive machine with plenty of power provided by a 250 hp Rolls-Royce engine.

Great things were expected of it and it was, eventually, able to deliver, when the technique for using it effectively was established, but on that first patrol led by Captain W. Leefe Robinson, the six Bristols ran into Richthofen's Jagdstaffel which shot down four and seriously damaged a fifth. Two of the four were downed by Richthofen himself and one of the four victims was Leefe Robinson.

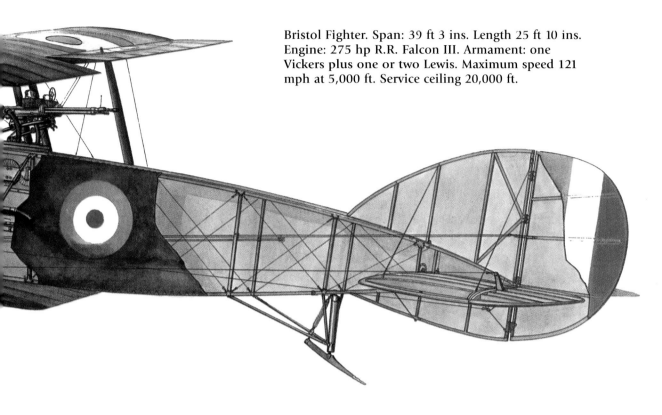

Bristol Fighter. Span: 39 ft 3 ins. Length 25 ft 10 ins. Engine: 275 hp R.R. Falcon III. Armament: one Vickers plus one or two Lewis. Maximum speed 121 mph at 5,000 ft. Service ceiling 20,000 ft.

Devil-may-care, Leefe Robinson was already a war hero having been awarded a VC for shooting down a Zeppelin over England. Mrs. Ward of Repton, Derbyshire, knew him and I was able to chat to her about him. She told me that he was a handsome young man of enormous charm, fanatically keen on flying. She also told me that he pronounced Leefe not as Leaf but as Leff.

His Bristol Fighter had been hit but he survived the crash to spend the war as a prisoner only to end it in poor health. Sadly he died in the dreadful influenza epidemic only a few weeks after the end of hostilities.

The ebullient Major HD Hervey-Kelly was one of the great characters of the RFC. He was in command of 19 Squadron and both Sholto and Lionel Blaxland knew him. Hervey-Kelly had the distinction of piloting the first aircraft to land in France on August 13th 1914, a BE2B.

One of the most open-hearted and gregarious of men with a tremendous sense of humour, he was an outstanding personality even compared to so many incredible characters within the RFC. Cecil Lewis who wrote the unforgettable account of flying in WW1, *Sagittarius Rising*, was in Hervey-Kelly's squadron in 1916 and recalled his announcement that the squadron was to throw a tremendous party. He arrived from Amiens "with a case of whisky, a case of Chardonnay and a large bath sponge!"

But Hervey-Kelly's luck ran out before the end of April 1917.

His squadron had been re-equipped with Spad VIIs.....sturdy, attractive machines, a French design that would not have looked out of place in the nineteen thirties. On April 29th on a morning patrol with two other aircraft he saw a large formation of Richthofen's Albatros fighters below him.

Although outnumbered the three Spads dived onto the Germans but all three were shot down. Hervey-Kelly survived but was badly wounded and a few days later he died from his wounds.

On the same day that Hervey-Kelly was shot down Richthofen destroyed five British machines, with his brother Lothar flying with him.

The very next day signalled a tremendous change in German tactics and they now flew in massed formations with many more planes than they had previously used. This was the first appearance of what was inevitably called 'Richthofen's Circus'. This departure, with big formations varying in size as required, was to continue for the rest of the war and be repeated again during the Second World War with the British 'Big Wings' making offensive sweeps over occupied France.

Sopwith Triplane.

9

MICK MANNOCK, THE TOP SCORING BRITISH PILOT

When I had the opportunity to talk to Lionel Blaxland I was most anxious to ask him about Mannock. Lionel knew Edward 'Mick' Mannock right from the start of his career when he arrived at 40 Squadron and before he had scored a single victory.

Mick Mannock went on to become the most successful British pilot of the war with, reputedly 73 victories so what sort of a man was he in those early days as a tyro fighter pilot?

"Well," replied Lionel, "Mick was a complex character. A difficult man to get to know and a difficult man to like, though those first impressions mellowed as I got to know him better.

"In appearance he was tall, slim, dark and with an incredible air of vitality, expressed by his clear, startlingly blue eyes." From what others have written he was well liked by the fair sex though never romantically involved.

Mick Mannock VC DSO (two bars) MC (one bar).

"What you must remember," said Lionel, "is that at thirty years old, having worked overseas and being held prisoner by the Turks, he was very much a man of the world. The rest of us, by comparison, were still wet behind the ears. I am sure that I was only about nineteen years old at the time."

He was a Socialist and from "the other side of the tracks" which rather put him at odds with his colleagues who were, in the main, drawn from the officer class. "It was," said Lionel, "no doubt difficult at first for him to fit into this new milieu." His fellow pilots, however, made him welcome right from the start.

He despised "snobbery" with particular hatred focused on "useless society women" and men of privileged social position with the advantage of a good school and university who used their 'contacts' to secure cushy jobs at home or behind the lines overseas. "It was every man's duty," he said, "to pull his weight in the war".

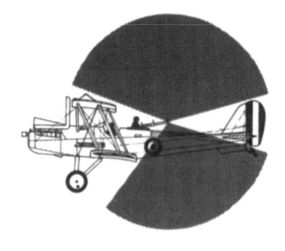

"Look out for the Hun in the Sun" – A First World War saying that was just as true in the Second.

Arcs of fire available to a two-seater 360° above. Either side below.

He also had a burning hatred for the Germans which was unusual in his fellow pilots. His colleagues, though determined to shoot down as many Germans as possible, also respected them as fellow aviators. They certainly did not hate them with Mick Mannock's incandescent intensity.

He was older than his colleagues and at thirty years of age was considered too old for a fighter pilot. With time he did fit in and gain acceptance.

As he gained confidence he loved discussion and argument, never backward in pressing the socialist cause. He became an enthusiastic after-dinner speaker in the mess, honing the debating skills he had learned in the Parliamentary Debating Society at Wellingborough. "He had," said Lionel, "a very pleasant speaking voice with the hint of an Irish accent."

Edward Mannock was born on May 1st 1887. His father was a professional soldier and had met his wife, Irish girl Julia O'Sullivan, while serving in Ireland. He also served in Egypt, India and in South Africa during the Boer War.

Young Edward was with his family in India for about six years from when he was six years old and started his "scanty education" at the Army school there.

After the Boer War, Corporal Mannock, as he then was, re-joined his family of two boys and three girls in England but then, unaccountably, he abandoned his family and never supported them again. His wife, Julia, with the scanty earnings of the two eldest children was faced with the daunting task of keeping the family together.

Mick was twelve years old when his father left but soon had to go to work to help his mother. Errand boy for a greengrocer first, working ten hour days for a wage of 2s6d (12$^1/_2$p) per week and next a barber's assistant at double the money. A step up, then, as a clerk in a telegraph company. The indoor job, however, began to affect his health so he moved to Wellingborough, Northants, as a linesman, a job that suited him well.

It was there that Mick started to blossom. He enjoyed a happy social life and lodged with Mr and Mrs Eyles who became his staunchest friends. He joined the Parliamentary Debating

Society and became the secretary of the local Labour Club.

In February 1914 he set his sights higher and with the help of some money lent to him by Mr Eyles and his brother he sailed to Turkey in a tramp steamer in the hope of a better job. He was taken on by an English telegraph company as an outdoor engineer and within six months was promoted to district inspector.

So he was on his way at last, wasn't he?

No he wasn't! The outbreak of war smashed his hopes and he was to remain bitterly resentful of Germany who started the war.

Turkey, of course, threw in her lot with Germany so Mick was interned. His life was at its lowest ebb but on April 1st 1915 his luck changed. He was repatriated with a batch of other prisoners on the grounds of age, poor health and defective eyesight as he had a congenital defect causing astigmatism (preventing proper focusing) in his left eye. The Turks thought that such a crock would be of no use to the British war effort…how wrong they were.

Back in England he joined the Royal Army Medical Corps then the Royal Engineers but his driving ambition was to be with the Royal Flying Corps and in August 1916 he managed it.

But how did he get away with that dodgy left eye when the official requirement was 100% eyesight in both eyes? Possibly the medical officer examining him uncovered the sight board for a few seconds and in those few seconds he managed to memorise the data, but whatever the reason, Mannock was accepted.

When he progressed to flying training one of his instructors was Jimmy McCudden who was to go on to become one of the highest scoring pilots of the war with 57 victories.

They both came from similar backgrounds: both were of Irish descent, both born within the service and both educated in army schools. They were clearly kindred spirits and became great friends. Mick Mannock, too, like Lionel Blaxland, flew DH2s and FE8s before leaving for France on March 3rd 1917.

Army Form W.3348.

COMBATS IN THE AIR

Squadron No.: 40. Date: 7.6.17.
Type and No. of Aeroplane: Time: 7.10–7.15.
  Nieuport Scout B.1552. Duty: Escort.
Armament: 1 Lewis Gun. Height: 13,000 ft.
Pilot: Lieutenant Mannock. Locality: North of Lille.
Observer: Nil.

RESULT : Destroyed .... Nil.
              Driven down out of control.. One.
              Driven down................ Nil.

Remarks on Hostile machine: Type, armament, speed, etc.: Single-seater Scout.

Narrative

When escorting machines N. of Lille one H.A. attempted to dive on one of the leading F.E.s but turned before diving. Nieuport engaged H.A. at very close range and fired approx. 30 rounds into pilot's position, and engine of H.A.

H.A. turned upside-down, nose-dived and spun, obviously out of control.

Nieuport endeavoured to watch H.A. crash, but was unable to do so.

Signed .... E. Mannock, 2/Lt.
This was witnessed by 2/Lt. Blaxland and 2/Lt. Lemon.
Signed .... G. W. Beer, R.O.,
Captain,
for O.C., No. 40 Squadron, R.F.C.

Mannock's first victory. Witnessed by 2nd Lieutenants Blaxland and Lemon. This is a copy of his combat report. 7/6/17.

The Kaiser Wilhelm II. Flattering picture of the man who started it all. His mother was the daughter of Queen Victoria which gave him an ambivalent view of Britain.

Cartoon showing the Kaiser racing towards Paris with the winged figure of Victory beside him. Fortunately the reality was different thanks to men like Mannock.

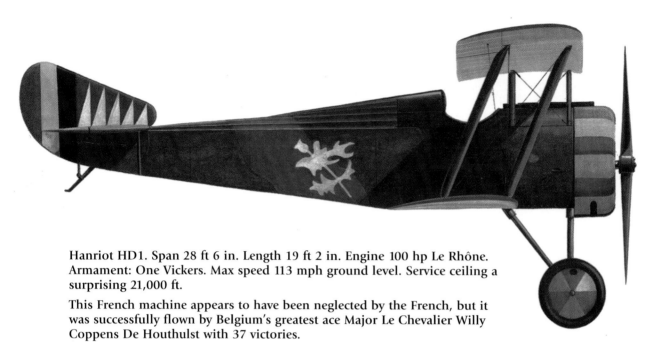

Hanriot HD1. Span 28 ft 6 in. Length 19 ft 2 in. Engine 100 hp Le Rhône. Armament: One Vickers. Max speed 113 mph ground level. Service ceiling a surprising 21,000 ft.

This French machine appears to have been neglected by the French, but it was successfully flown by Belgium's greatest ace Major Le Chevalier Willy Coppens De Houthulst with 37 victories.

On April 19th 1917 Mick Mannock was on machine-gun practise diving steeply onto the ground target when the bottom plane of his Nieuport broke away. Sholto Douglas saw this happen and this is his description.

"My attention was drawn to Mick Mannock one afternoon shortly after his arrival at Treizennes, and it was in a fashion that was somewhat spectacular. I was standing with some of my pilots by one of our squadron hangars and we were watching one of the Nieuports of No. 40 Squadron swooping down onto a ground target used for practise firing on the range near the aerodrome. I noticed that the pilot – who was Mannock, although I did not know that at the time – appeared to be diving the Nieuport rather more steeply and fiercely than was usual. As he started to pull out of the dive the lower plane of his aircraft which was narrower and shorter than the top plane, buckled and fell away. By all the laws that govern such events, that Nieuport should have gone plummeting into the ground, but Mannock, fully aware of what had happened, coolly throttled back his engine and managed, by first-rate flying and supported only by his top plane, to glide gently down into a field alongside our own airfield. Inexperienced though he was, Mannock showed in that one incident that he was certainly made of the right stuff".

Up until June 1917 Mannock, though in many combats, failed to score an official victory though he would often return with his machine shot about and thought he had decisively hit enemy planes.

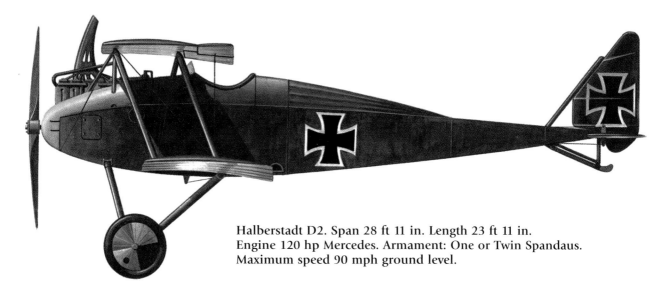

Halberstadt D2. Span 28 ft 11 in. Length 23 ft 11 in.
Engine 120 hp Mercedes. Armament: One or Twin Spandaus.
Maximum speed 90 mph ground level.

During that time he often discussed his lack of success with Lionel who did his best to keep Mannock's spirits up. On June 7th 1917, however, Mick Mannock's luck changed and this victory was witnessed by Lionel and Lemon. A copy of the combat report is included on page 57. The entry in Lionel's log book for that date can be found in Chapter One.

I asked Lionel about this combat and he remembered it very clearly. "After this breakthrough," he said, "I was certain that Mick would now get into his stride."

Back from leave in July Mannock really did get into his stride, starting off with two two-seaters down on July 12th and 13th. MC on July 22nd, then promoted to captain and then he became a flight commander.

His victories continued to mount up and on October 4th 1917 he was awarded a bar to his MC. By the time he left 40 Squadron to return home on January 2nd 1918 his score stood at 23.

We know that Lionel had his Lewis gun set to fire along the line of flight of his aircraft, though this did not apply to everyone. It was well-known, however, that Mannock looked after his own Lewis gun, so did he, too, set it up to fire along the line of flight?

I asked Lionel about this but he couldn't be sure, though he was under the impression that Mannock's gun, too, was set to fire along the line of flight.

Kipling wrote:
> *When you're wounded and lie on Afghanistan plains*
> *And the women come out to cut up what remains*
> *Just roll to your rifle and blow out your brains*
> *And go to your God like a soldier.*

Death was inevitable anyway but by pulling that trigger the soldier would deny the Afghan women the pleasure of torturing him and avoid a dreadful death. It's chilling to think that British soldiers are still being killed in Afghanistan today. But what has this got to do with Mick

Mannock, I hear you ask? I will explain. Many 1914 – 1918 airmen have written about the horror they felt when they saw a fellow aviator, British or German, falling to his death in a blazing aircraft. Mick Mannock had a phobia about facing such a death and always kept his service revolver clean and oiled ready to put a bullet through his brain if he ever encountered such a fate.

He made no secret about this and spoke to Lionel about it several times. The first that Lionel knew about this was when he called in on Mannock's hut and found him cleaning his revolver. "If my plane ever goes down in flames, Blax," he said, "this is the answer." He nodded towards his revolver.

10

BILL BOND

Derbyshire man William Arthur 'Bill' Bond had served in the infantry in France and Gallipoli where he had won the Military Cross for bringing in a wounded comrade while under withering enemy fire.

He joined the RFC in 1916 and, like Lionel Blaxland, went for his initial training at Netheravon then to Upavon where they met. He was awarded his wings on November 23rd at Upavon then proceeded onto further training before joining 40 Squadron at Treizennes in early April 1917.

They were all individualists in 40 Squadron but Lionel described Bill as an exceptionally likeable man who was "always writing"! He was fortunate to have joined the squadron when it had just been re-equipped with Nieuport 17s, replacing the FE8 deathtraps.

Before the war Bill had been a journalist, eventually moving to Paris and becoming the sub-editor at the Daily Mail. He was a *bon viveur*, thoroughly enjoying life in Paris and

Bill Bond. Photograph from *Fighter Pilot* by McScotch.

travelling extensively through Europe. He met kindred spirit Aimée McHardy and they embarked upon an all-consuming love affair. They married in January 1917.

Aimée was also a journalist and after Bill's death she wrote a compelling account of their love affair including their wartime correspondence. Bill's letters have given us a unique insight into the life and times of a fighter pilot in 40 Squadron.[1]

1. Aimée's book, *An Airman's Wife*, was published in early 1918 and became a best seller. Derbyshire writer and aviation historian Barry M. Marsden had it re-published in 2005 by Grub Street.

Bill met Herbert Edward Ellis (also 'Bill') in Gallipoli and they became great friends. He, too, was decorated in Gallipoli. They were re-united when both of them were undergoing flying training at Upavon and both were honeymooning on Salisbury Plain at the same time. They met up, yet again, at Treizennes where Bill Ellis had joined 40 Squadron just a few days before Bill Bond.

By the time the two Bills arrived at the squadron there was a new CO, Major Leonard Arthur Tilney, MC. Despite his modest twenty-two years he was already 'blooded' as a wartime pilot. Bill Bond described him as "a tousle headed youth in pyjamas and flying coat… who could never restrain his blushes."

Bill's first forays over the lines were uneventful other than the inevitable baptism of fire by 'Archie'. His first encounter with the enemy was on April 22nd 1917 when on an offensive patrol with his pal Bill Ellis and a man named Mackenzie. Diving down onto a two-seater reconnaissance plane his Lewis gun, predictably, jammed whereupon the German turned to attack him and he had to take avoiding action.

Bill Bond in a Nieuport.

On the same afternoon the same three crossed the lines again and attacked a pair of German two-seaters. Bill fired several bursts and was sure he had hit the observer before his gun jammed again. Once again the German turned to attack him and again he had to take avoiding action.

A subsequent member of Bill's flight, Lt. William MacLanachan, (McScotch) described him thus: "He was English, a correspondent on one of the daily papers. He spent a good deal of his time writing and there was frequently a good deal of discussion between him and the CO as to what would pass the censor. He was about five feet seven or eight, had a cheery smile and did everything with an unassuming air that increased everyone's admiration."

The next day Bill recorded the achievements of 40 Squadron pilots, Brewis and Napier who, assisted by a Sopwith Triplane, forced down a DFW CV two-seater to land at Le Fagon, near Béthune, ten miles on the British side of the lines. The captured plane was then flown to the squadron airfield at Treizennes.

On April 25th the squadron left Treizennes for Auchel where "everything is upset and uncomfortable".

Bill's new flight commander arrived from England, Captain F.L. Barwell who had been his instructor in England. Sadly Barwell only lasted a few days and was shot down and killed on April 29th.

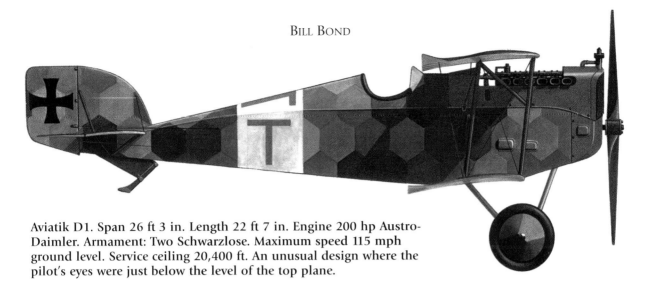

Aviatik D1. Span 26 ft 3 in. Length 22 ft 7 in. Engine 200 hp Austro-Daimler. Armament: Two Schwarzlose. Maximum speed 115 mph ground level. Service ceiling 20,400 ft. An unusual design where the pilot's eyes were just below the level of the top plane.

The squadron moved to Bruay on the 29th and Bill and J.G. Brewis, who had helped to drive down the DFW, set out on patrol. They became separated in thick mist. Bill managed to land at an airfield forty miles away but Brewis never returned and was posted missing.

On May 2nd the 40 Squadron pilots went 'Balloon busting'…. a notoriously dangerous mission as the balloons were protected by deadly machine-gun nests and heavier guns firing the notorious 'flaming onions'. Bill returned with his machine damaged and the engine gave up as he reached the airfield, necessitating a forced landing, but he was unhurt.

Five balloons were destroyed. It would have been six but Mackenzie's machine-gun jammed. No less than the commander-in-chief of the BEF General Douglas Haig sent a message to Major Tilney applauding the squadron on: "A very fine performance. Please congratulate those that carried out the attack on the great success of their efforts."

On May 6th Bill with Gregory and Mackenzie attacked two Rumplers at 16,000ft east of Henin-Liétard. Bill attacked the second firing 50 rounds at 100 yards and the Rumpler dived steeply away. A British artillery position saw the combat and reported that one of the Germans had crashed. Bill wrote to Aimee, "We don't know which of us it was, but think, me."

On the same morning, Bill's friend Bill Ellis, with seven victories to his credit, crash-landed. He hit his head and, sadly, lost most of his memory. He was taken to hospital but Bill told Aimee that he had completely forgotten the war. He vaguely remembered London and recognised his wife's photograph. He remained in hospital, still with a damaged memory, but nothing is known of what happened to him afterwards.

On May 7th Bill was balloon busting again but withering machine-gun fire forced him to break off. Six of the seven balloons were destroyed but newcomer, Captain Eric Dixon, another Derbyshire man, was missing.

On May 10th Bill and Gregory climbed to over 16,000ft over Hunland then dived down to attack two Aviatik two-seaters. Bill emptied his drum into one of them and it went down in a spinning dive. It was confirmed down at Sailly en Ostravent.

On May 11th Bill led his first patrol but endured extremely heavy anti-aircraft fire. So heavy, in fact, that the black, oily shellbursts blotted out his companions. Bill's plane was hit and the right aileron control shot away. Bill, however, found that he could still make low speed turns and managed to slide to a stop at the airfield.

The pilots were desperate for a respite but patrols continued. On May 13th Bill, Gregory and Godfrey headed out on "the most uncomfortable patrol I have ever had". The three pilots dived onto an enemy two-seater which fired three signal rockets….a trap! Two Albatros fighters stooped down onto Bill with Spandaus blazing.

Bill jinked like a snipe "never going straight for three seconds together". He managed to cross the lines unscathed when his attackers gave up the chase. Gregory and Godfrey also got back safely.

On May 26th the squadron held a farewell party for Bill's flight commander, Captain William Robert Gregory MC, Legion d'Honneur.

He was the son of Sir William and Lady Augusta Gregory of County Galway and was probably the pilot who forced down Richthofen on March 9th 1917.

William Gregory was Harrow and Oxford educated, a talented boxer and cricketer, keen rider to hounds and a promising painter and designer. He had married in 1907 and had two daughters.

His service in 40 Squadron had commenced in August 1916. And he had survived. No mean achievement. He went on to command 66 Squadron flying Sopwith Camels but was killed in action serving with his unit in Italy in January 1918.

Bill described him as "an awfully dear fellow and absolutely the stoutest-hearted I have ever met. He is thirty-five and married." Thirty-five was, of course, considered to be very old for a pilot in those days.

FE 2B France. From left to right: Godfrey, Kennedy, Mannock and Bond.

11
THE AIR WAR INTENSIFIES

The young, high-spirited pilots in the First World War were, without doubt, a remarkable crowd. Individualists to a man. Some, of course, were even more remarkable than others and among them was John Lewis Morgan, the Air Hog. He was fanatically keen to head out over the lines and attack the enemy.

Bill Bond wrote, "He was simply crazy to get Huns… He went out a few times and then developed a habit of going up and tearing about the sky all alone. He went Hun strafing mad….At last he was put on the roving commission game and since then has spent eight hours a day at least in the air. When it is not fit for patrol he mopes and frets, and worries everybody about the weather."

For a month the Air Hog roamed the skies attacking anything and everything that came his way. On the May 2nd balloon strafe he flew alongside the parachute of a baled out German observer and doubtless scared the unfortunate man witless by making faces at him!

The Air Hog. Lieutenant John Lewis Morgan was fantastically keen to shoot down the enemy. *(Hal Giblin Collection)*

He was awarded the Military Cross for his "general keenness and good work" but shortly afterwards his career was halted when his Nieuport was hit by an anti-aircraft shell which blew out part of the Le Rhône engine, destroyed the undercarriage and riddled his legs with shrapnel. Despite his severe injuries he managed to glide across the lines and crashed. His right leg was amputated below the knee yet two hours later he was writing to his parents to reassure them.

Bill wrote, "I don't think many people so well deserved an MC." He went on, "No more jolly old patrols for him." But Bill was wrong. He recovered and with an artificial leg he re-joined the RFC early in 1918 and served as aerial flight instructor to 50 Squadron in Kent.

On April 26th that year the engine of his SE5 failed on take-off and, like Jimmy McCudden later, he made the fatal mistake of attempting to turn back to the airfield. His plane side-slipped into a nosedive and he was killed. A tragic end to a gallant airman.

Another larger than life character in 40 Squadron was 'The Haystack Expert', alias 'The Hun',

John Lancashire Barlow. On his first flight with the squadron he managed to hit a pile of straw on take-off and that's how he got the first nickname. Two days later he took off safely but on landing he rocketed between a hangar and some cottages ending up with his plane on its nose in a sunken road. He was promptly re-christened 'The Hun'!

On June 9th he encountered a flight of red Albatros fighters, without doubt part of Richthofen's Jasta. He shot down one and another was recorded as 'out of control'. His own machine was riddled with 58 bullet holes and was a write-off. Barlow, however, had amply demonstrated his fighting spirit though his score to date was two German fighters to three Nieuports!

A colleague later recalled that "he treated the war as if it was really a 'rag' on a stupendous scale". He went on to score six victories with the squadron but on September 23rd he was shot down and killed, aged 18.

On May 27th 1917 Bill Bond was a temporary flight commander and led a high altitude flight protecting photo-reconnaissance two-seaters. On his third sortie of the day with Lt. Godfrey he attacked a number of Albatros fighters flying above him then on his return he attacked four Albatros fighters below him.

The 28th was packed with action: 40's Nieuports were in combat with several Albatros Jastas. Bill claimed two Albatri down and a British fighter from another squadron shot an Albatros off Bill's tail. Bill's Lewis gun was jammed at the time. As a result of this Major Tilney recommended Bill for a bar to his MC for his "remarkably good and conscientious work".

About this time Bill was getting worried by his spate of clumsy landings, having damaged

BE2E being started in France 1917.

DFW Aviatik (220 Benz) driven down near Béthune, May 1917 by Lts Brewis and Napier of 40 Squadron.

DFW Aviatik.

his tail skids on landing five times. This was considered to be due to the effect of flying at such high altitudes without oxygen. Bill was not alone. A number of other pilots faced the same problem.

On June 1st Bill, Godfrey and Lancashire were returning from a patrol when Bill and Godfrey saw British anti-aircraft fire bursting around an aircraft. Bill closed behind the aircraft and with finger on the trigger was just about to fire when he realised that it was a British Sopwith Triplane. It was probably an RNAS aircraft from nearby Mont St. Eloi and the British gunners had fired on it by mistake.

On June 4th, Bill, Tilney and Mannock took off at 4am hoping to intercept a German plane that had flown over the airfield at high altitude for four mornings running but on this day it failed to turn up.

At 9.30am on the same morning he was off again escorting photo-reconnaissance aircraft. The same evening Captain Allcock headed a line patrol with Bill leading a sub-section of three Nieuports. At 16,000 ft they saw a flight of a dozen German fighters 2,000ft below them: "No two were alike and hardly one machine was painted all the same colour; green wings and red fuselages; pink and purple; yellow tails and white and black wings. They were hideous."

Both German and British machines manoeuvred in an attempt to gain advantage but, in the end, running low on fuel, Allcock had to turn back for home.

On the evening of June 5th Bill was in "a hell of a scrap". Flight commander Allcock suggested patrolling the same area as the previous day but Shaw and Maclennan had to turn back with faulty engines leaving four machines to continue.

Bill saw five Albatros D3s to the east above him with four below. Bill and Allcock dived onto the lower machines and downed them both. Bill then dived onto another four Albatri but his gun jammed after 25 rounds. He then dived away, heading for home, with two Albatri hard on his tail. Redler and Gordon arrived back safely and confirmed Bill and Allcock's victories, but Allcock failed to return.

On June 7th the next 'Big Push' on Messines Ridge started preceded by a tremendous barrage. Bill flew as part of a bomber escort and passed over "a patch of country about twenty miles long and twelve miles deep, just ablaze…. It was so stupid and senseless." Many other airmen must have echoed his thoughts. He went on to write that the bombardment had left "a smoking, churned, shell-pocked, brown belt of destroyed country behind it". As he flew at 12,000ft over the carnage he thanked "some of my gods that I was no longer a landsman in combat".

Three German fighters swooped down, unseen by Bill and one got onto his tail. Fortunately, Godfrey, Bill's right hand man, did see the German and fired eighty rounds into it, shooting it down. Bill pursued another Albatros but without result.

Bill wrote to Aimée about Godfrey describing him as his "right hand man on patrol…wonderfully reliable. He's a Canadian and talks it violently and nasally – when he does talk, which is rare. Usually he is very quiet. But when he is excited – say when he comes back from a scrap – nothing holds him. His language, all unconsciously, is lurid."

Captain (later Group Captain) Albert Earl 'Steve' Godfrey claimed 14 victories in WWI and died in 1982 aged 92.

On the evening of June 9th Bill led a line patrol and at 15,000ft saw an enemy two-seater

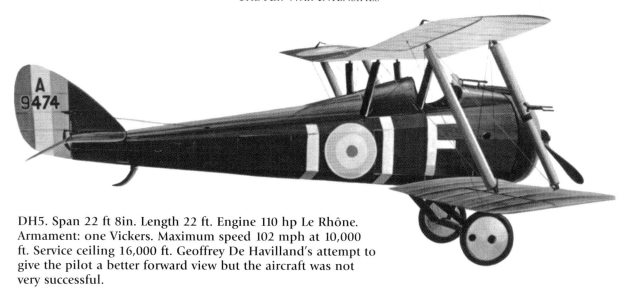

DH5. Span 22 ft 8in. Length 22 ft. Engine 110 hp Le Rhône. Armament: one Vickers. Maximum speed 102 mph at 10,000 ft. Service ceiling 16,000 ft. Geoffrey De Havilland's attempt to give the pilot a better forward view but the aircraft was not very successful.

2,000ft below. He dived down then swooped up below the aircraft to avoid the observer's fire but the enemy pilot opened his throttle and shot away, at the same time firing a signal flare.

Bill swung round in a wide circle, arriving back at the point where he had seen the two-seater and, sure enough, five enemy fighters were below him. Bill dived onto the last one while Mick Mannock and Mac Blaxland attacked two of the others. Bill's would-be victim spotted him and rocketed away to join his companions. Bill saw the enemy leader break away and swing round to climb above him so he abandoned his original target and headed off his new opponent, firing 40 rounds into him. The Albatros turned onto its back and went down out of control. This was witnessed by other members of his patrol.

Bill then zoomed up hard and fired at another Albatros until it broke away then fired twenty rounds from his near-empty drum into yet another Albatros. He was sure that he had hit them both but without inflicting vital damage. Bill saw more opponents well to the east and above him but decided it was time to head for home.

His successes were enthusiastically received by his fellow pilots and he wrote: "Why it was such a nice scrap was that we always remained level with or above the Huns. Not one of them ever got his sights on me to fire, and I'd a Hun to go at every time I looked for one."

June 1917 continued to be a busy month for Bill. On the 12th he twice pursued German two-seaters but without success. That night he dined with 10 Squadron as they were moving to another airfield. On the 26th Bill led another patrol and they were very annoyed when a hostile machine sailed over them while they were climbing up on the British side of the lines. They attempted pursuit but without success. Finally over the lines they attacked a two-seater. Bill and Lemon managed to fire at it but without result and it dived away into the haze.

On the same day Bill and his friend Hubert Redler flew to Lozinghem for lunch with 43 Squadron who, as already mentioned, flew Sopwith 1^1/$_2$ Strutters. On the same day the news came through that Redler had been awarded the MC. Bill wrote to Aimée: "He is my right hand man. He always flies close behind me, and I always know he will be there."

June 21st saw Bill, Godfrey and Redler on an uneventful early line patrol. Later in the day he flew to the RNAS airfield at Mont St. Eloi to give a demonstration flight for HQ staff. "I just did everything I could think of and then came home," wrote Bill.

On the 24th he led an early patrol with five colleagues and at 16,000 feet saw six biplanes "of the new Albatros type" which were, presumably, the new D5s which had started to arrive at the front during the previous month. The Albatri were about 2,000 ft above them but Godfrey managed to get on the tail of one of them and sent it down out of control. F.W. Rook also managed to drive down another but Bill was unable to engage them.

On June 26th Bill flew out of the advanced landing ground at Mazingarbe and chased a two-seater but without success. Later in the day he fired 50 rounds at a balloon which was winched down.

On June 29th on an afternoon patrol he saw six red Albatros fighters south-east of Ypres and eight more of the same north east of the town. Bill and Godfrey attacked the lower formation, firing at long range but without success. Bill then wrote to Aimée saying that he had been promised command of A flight and promotion to captain. "I so much wanted B flight," he wrote, "and all the fellows in it and the personnel wanted me to have it, too." Leave was due the following week.

Bill and Aimée enjoyed a marvellous few days together from July 2nd to 19th. They played golf together by the sea, visited his parents at Chesterfield and spent an evening in London with Gregory, Godfrey and Lemon.

DH5.

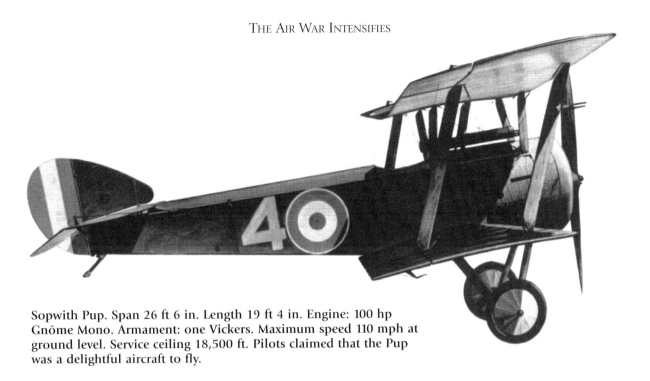

Sopwith Pup. Span 26 ft 6 in. Length 19 ft 4 in. Engine: 100 hp
Gnôme Mono. Armament: one Vickers. Maximum speed 110 mph at
ground level. Service ceiling 18,500 ft. Pilots claimed that the Pup
was a delightful aircraft to fly.

Mono 'Pup'.

12

BACK FROM LEAVE

Bill Bond flew back on July 19th 1917 in a new type of fighter, presumably a Sopwith Camel. It took half an hour to start it then he spent twenty minutes taxying it round the airfield to get used to it.

He found it difficult to get the air/fuel mixture right and when he did take off the engine failed to give full power. He limped along despite the engine giving up twice, though he managed to re-start it. Was the plane trying to tell him something? Despite all this he did get the machine across the Channel and landed safely in France.

Back to the squadron by motorcycle and sidecar, no doubt an RFC P&M, he was welcomed back by Major Tilney and Padre Keymer who were playing tennis. Bill and four fellow pilots then took a tender to town to round off the day with an enjoyable meal.

MacLanachan wrote: "Bond's promotion was popular, and on his return there was a great celebration in the squadron." Mannock had just been awarded the MC and Bill wrote: "Though his judgement was not always good he is absolutely without fear and does his job always." A fascinating insight.

The next day Bill led his patrol over the lines and, like so many pilots after a leave, found getting back into the swing of things surprisingly difficult. He wrote; "I couldn't feel the machine properly and I couldn't tell where I was." The patrol ran into heavy anti-aircraft fire but no enemy aircraft were encountered.

On July 21st Bill wrote to his wife for the last time. He told Aimée about an evening patrol where B Flight acted as decoys for four other Nieuports patrolling above them. They were flying at 15,000ft when nine enemy fighters appeared from an easterly direction. Only Mannock and Bill saw them and manoeuvred to get within range. Five of the enemy planes passed below them but Bill dared not attack as two more Albatri were seen above them. Finally, with fuel running low, they were forced to turn for home.

On Sunday July 22nd Bill led the dawn patrol. The five planes were in an arrowhead formation with MacLanachan on Bill's left, about forty feet away.

MacLanachan wrote: "Bond was not the type that bothered much whether the patrol was officially 'line' or 'offensive'. There was only one type for A Flight and as soon as we got over the trenches it was apparent that not only was our patrol going to be offensive but that 'aggressively belligerent' would describe it more aptly."

A Sopwith Pup. Engine bearers collapsed whilst machine was in flight, two cylinders were torn off but pilot got machine into aerodrome without further damage.

No enemy aircraft were sighted but west of Douai, six miles behind the lines, a kite balloon came into view. Bill rocked his wings and dived onto the "Dirty, inflated, bulbous sausage". For some reason, however, Bill only fired a few rounds before breaking away and heading back towards the lines at about 80mph and at 8,000ft.

Suddenly a quartet of shells burst among the Nieuports and MacLanachan saw Bill's machine disappear among the oily, black shellbursts. MacLanachan wrote: "Pieces of aeroplane fabric were whirling crazily in the air amidst the huge black smoke balls of the Archie bursts." He looked round frantically for Bill but " all that remained in the air were the stupid, dancing remnants of his planes."

Bill and his Nieuport had suffered a direct hit and both had been blown to pieces. Redler's Nieuport, too, had been hit and the engine cowling torn off. He managed to cross the lines, however, and crash-landed on the shell-pocked ground behind them.

Engine after bearers had given way. Sopwith Pup (Mono).

MacLanachan had long predicted that the deadly AA batteries near La Bassée or between the River Scarpe and Quiery would, one day, score a direct hit with their opening salvo. He wrote: "Poor Bond, had his enthusiasm possibly made him forgetful of this ever-present danger?"

Bill Bond's tragic death hit the squadron hard. MacLanachan wrote that it, "filled us with consternation. The fact that the indomitable Bond had been killed by a direct hit from Archie meant more to us even than the loss of a friend." What made the loss even worse for MacLanachan was that he "had been within forty feet of my Flight Commander when his machine was shattered in a savage, black, shell-burst." Even Major Tilney who usually did his utmost to keep up squadron morale "succumbed to the general depression".

Bill and his friend Hubert Redler had agreed that if either of them was killed the survivor would write to the next of kin and pack up all the deceased's belongings to return to his family. Hubert Redler commenced this melancholy task while MacLanachan "sat on Bond's bed sorting out his belongings, his books, his clothes, his manuscript; and when I came to his shaving kit and a few delicate souvenirs of his happiness with his wife, the terrible loneliness of us all was amply impressed on my mind."

Aimée was distraught by Bill's death and, in fact, refused to accept it for many weeks, clinging to the impossible hope that somehow he had survived. In September, however, the Army Council wrote to Bill's father pointing out that as there was no further news on his 'missing' status they were "regretfully constrained to conclude that he was killed in action on that date."

Bill was officially credited with five victories plus a balloon but, of course, in addition to that, there were a substantial number of 'probables'. He has no known grave but he is listed on the Arras Flying Services Memorial which commemorates the men of the RFC who fell in the battle. It was unveiled by Lord Trenchard in 1932. The Germans must have had some evidence of his identity as their casualty schedule for July listed his name.

Aimée's best seller *An Airman's Wife* must have helped her, in some small measure, to endure his loss. She wrote:

> *On that Sunday morning your life went out "into the ether" and you left me here.*
> *From higher than the highest hill you came spinning down.*
> *Your body, that belonged to me, must have made a big hole in the ground.*
> *And I, who could have rendered living beautiful for you, even if you had been crippled,*
> *or disfigured, or blinded, may not touch nor hear nor see you any more.*
> *My useless tears are falling.*

13

FLYING THE NIEUPORT 17

An essential question to ask Lionel Blaxland was: "What was it like to fly the Nieuport 17?"

This was the first tractor machine he had ever flown after the series of pushers. The Nieuport, he said, was a revelation: not only was it faster and with a far better rate of climb but he described it as so manoeuvrable and such a delight to fly. At last he had a machine that could compete with the Albatros.

It was an aircraft, he said, that was completely unstable. It had to be "flown" always and would not tolerate any lack of attention by the pilot. Relax for a moment and you would quickly lose control but that made it such a nimble machine to handle. Another advantage over the Albatros was the torque of the rotary engine which meant that you could out-turn your opponents by utilising the torque effect by turning in the same direction as the engine was spinning.

C Flight. Nieuport 17s ready to take off.

Lionel Blaxland's machine with "Fitter" and "Rigger", Wood and Bone.

LBB's machine.

So flying the Nieuport gave you the confidence that you could out-perform any plane that the Germans could throw at you. The ideal dog-fighting machine when the pilot had got used to it.

He pointed out that the fuel/air mixture was controlled by the pilot and altered as the altitude increased. In addition to that it varied between damp and dry conditions. It was all too easy to run the engine over-rich and choke it when it would cut out and then it required a long glide to spin the propeller and re-start it. But, once again, experience made all the difference as then you could "feel" that the mixture was right.

A curious thing was what Lionel told me about the sighting of the machine-gun on his Nieuport: As received from the factory, he said, the Lewis gun on the top wing was set to fire at an angle above the line of flight. (This was 15 degrees.) "But we always asked the mechanics to re-rig the gun with aero elastics to fire along the line of flight like the German Albatros." So there you have it though I have never seen this mentioned elsewhere. So Lionel's Nieuport and, it seems, those of some of his fellow pilots had their machine-guns firing in the line of flight.

He explained what an effort it was at high altitudes to haul down the Lewis to change the drum and that it was even harder to get it back up again. This was made even more difficult as you only had to change it when the enemy was shooting back at you. Difficult, too, to keep control of the skittish Nieuport when changing drums. On one occasion the drum slipped out of his hands and hit him an almighty crack on the head but, fortunately he kept control of the aircraft.

What I did find surprising was that neither Lionel nor many other pilots, as far as I know, complained about their lamentable lack of firepower compared to that of their opponents. Only 97 rounds then the drum had to be changed compared to the 1,000-round uninterrupted fire of the Albatros. But what they all did complain about, without exception, was the unreliability of their Lewis guns.

Reading the memoirs of the pilots of the time you encounter numerous instances of the guns jamming after only a few rounds had been fired. Lionel was no exception. Was this due to an inherent design fault or was it down to the quality of the ammunition? The .303 ammunition for aircraft was specially checked and checked again on the airfield, but the problems continued.

I once met a New Zealander who had been employed by the government to shoot red deer as their numbers had got out of hand. The New Zealand government at that time, after World War Two, were obviously very economy-minded. These rangers were issued with Long Lee Enfield rifles from about 1900, which they called 'Long Toms' and special ammunition that had been originally issued for aircraft use in World War One! How economical can you get?

14

ALBERT BALL
LEADS THE FIGHT BACK

Albert Ball was born in Nottingham in 1896 and on leaving school he set up his own electrical and brassfounding business. He joined the Army in 1914, transferring to the RFC in January 1916.

In France in February 1916 he was flying two-seater BE2Cs with 13 Squadron on reconnaissance and artillery spotting duties. He did briefly fly a Bristol scout and on May 11th he transferred to 11 Squadron flying Nieuport single-seater fighters.

Lionel Blaxland knew him and described him to me as a very pleasant character but with no hint of the fiery persona he assumed in the air.

He soon started to score, shooting down an Albatros D1 on May 22nd and on the same patrol forcing an LGV two-seater to land. Due to lack of witnesses neither of these victories was confirmed. However a balloon on June 25th and a Roland on July 2nd were confirmed.

He was under such pressure during the Battle of the Somme that he asked for a brief rest from combat flying but, to his disgust, he was sent to 8 Squadron flying BE2Cs again! Even so he continued to fly aggressively and on August 10th he was back in 11 Squadron.

From then on he really showed his mettle and on August 16th he attacked five enemy machines single-handed and shot down three of them. Five days later he went after seven Roland C2s, shooting down one and avoiding the fire of the others. He then attacked another five and shot two down.

His reputation as a devil-may-care pilot was now established. He would hurl his Nieuport 17, machine-gun blazing, into a German Jagdstaffel regardless of the odds. He would then shoot his way out, remaining unscathed. But, of course, these tactics could not have succeeded later in the war when the science of air fighting had evolved.

Some pilots never could get on with the nimble, fiery Nieuport 17s but others loved them: Albert Ball was one of the latter. Even when his squadron changed to the later SE5a, he was allowed to keep a Nieuport for his own use.

An advantage of the Lewis gun on the top plane was that it could be pulled down and fired vertically upwards. Ball was an exponent though Lionel Blaxland never mentioned using it in that way to me. Flying unseen under a German reconnaissance plane Ball would haul down his Lewis gun and fire a deadly burst into it to bring it down.

So why was this tactic so little used by other pilots? The reason was the 'put-salt-on-its-tail'

Albert Ball in his SE5a. *(Imperial War Museum.)*

LFG Roland C2. Span 33 ft 8 in. Length 25 ft 2 in. Engine 160 hp Mercedes. Armament: one Spandau, one 7.92 mm Parabellum. Maximum speed 103 mph. Service ceiling 13,100 ft. Full marks for this highly advanced streamlined biplane. Albert Ball stalked them with great success.

Nieuport taking off. Sorry about the poor quality, but photographs of planes in the air are so rare.

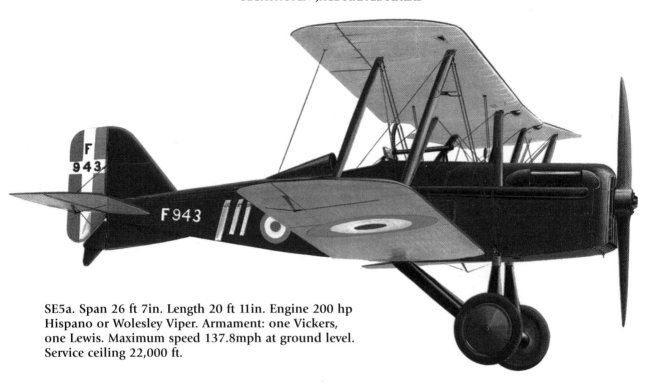

SE5a. Span 26 ft 7in. Length 20 ft 11in. Engine 200 hp
Hispano or Wolesley Viper. Armament: one Vickers,
one Lewis. Maximum speed 137.8mph at ground level.
Service ceiling 22,000 ft.

Hermann Göring and Bruno Loerzer were comrades in arms. They are standing in front of an
Albatros D5 in 1917. They commanded Jastas 27 and 26 and shared the same airfield.

1917. 'SE5' 200 Hispano Suiza. Lionel at Rochford.

DH4 400 hp Rolls. Could this be the 375 hp Eagle Vlll? Personal unknown.

Above: Lionel with unidentified single-seater fighter. Note the "Good Luck" swastika motif.

Opposite page: The same aircraft with Howe on the left but unidentified others. Note twin machine-guns and ring sight.

theory. To catch a rabbit you first put salt on its tail then grab it: the difficulty is getting close enough to the rabbit in the first place. The same problem applied to flying unseen under an enemy aircraft: the difficulty, again, was getting there in the first place.

He left France on October 4th having destroyed ten aircraft and forced down twenty but he found flying instruction in England far too tame and was back in France in April 1917 as a flight commander in the prestigious 56 Squadron, the first to be equipped with the new SE5as. Most pilots were delighted to change from Nieuports to SEs but not Ball. He much preferred the Nieuport though he flew them both.

Victories continued to accumulate and on May 6th flying his Nieuport he shot down an Albatros fighter of Jasta 20 using his salt-on-the-tail tactic by flying underneath it and firing upwards with his Lewis.

That was to be Albert Ball's last victory as on May 7th, late in the evening, he was seen diving his SE5 into dense cloud in pursuit of a German single-seater but nothing more is known. The Germans claimed that he was shot down by Lothar von Richthofen but Lothar said that the machine he had shot down was a Sopwith Triplane and this was confirmed by other witnesses. So Ball's death is shrouded in mystery.

Captain Collett – wounded in the hand over Houthulst Forest after shooting down two EA. He was killed accidently near the Forth Bridge, 23rd December 1917.

Avro in flight and Sopwith on ground. Rochford 1918.

BE2E after spinning into the ground. The pilot was very badly hurt.

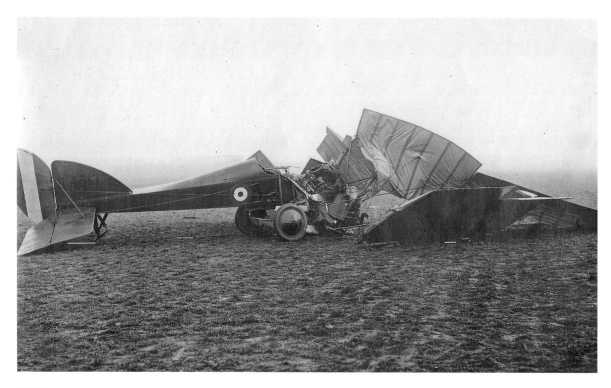

BE2E.

The two 260 hp Mercedes engines taken from the Gotha that crashed at Rochford, December 1917.

Albatros D5 at Rochford flown by Captain Clive Collett.

61 Squadron SEs.

The Sopwith Swallow. A rare bird. A monoplane using a Camel fuselage and 110 hp Le Rhône engine. It is believed that only one was made but the experiment was never taken any further.

The famous American Curtiss 'Jenny' two-seater, but author is unsure whether any were used operationally in the war. This one, however, appeared at Rochford.

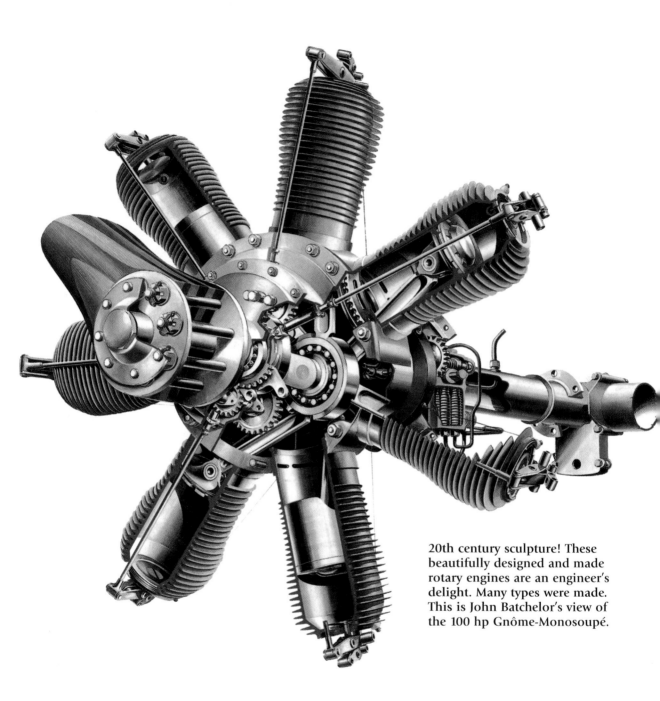

20th century sculpture! These beautifully designed and made rotary engines are an engineer's delight. Many types were made. This is John Batchelor's view of the 100 hp Gnôme-Monosoupé.

15

THE ENGINES

In the first part of the war the British favoured rotary engines but the Germans used in-line water-cooled engines: ugly looking brutes with their untidy, exposed valve gear. Ugly they may have been but they were both powerful and reliable. The introduction of the Fokker Triplane later in the war required a rotary Oberusel engine.

Rotaries seem strange to us today: the crankshaft stood still and the crankcase and cylinders spun round it! No, I'm not kidding. The propeller was bolted to the crankcase.

But the rotaries were really beautiful engines (see opposite). Difficult to understand this from a photograph but you will be in no doubt if you actually see one. They had to be superbly engineered, built and balanced to perfection otherwise they would have shaken themselves to pieces. Just look at those gleaming, machined steel-finned cylinders and you will instantly see what I mean.

The rotaries were very successful with an excellent power to weight ratio. Ignition to those spinning cylinders required careful design….and ingenuity, but it was successfully accomplished. It is fascinating to see them slowly turning over, driven by electric motors, in the London Science Museum.

The German in-line water-cooled engines were conventional, like the engines in a motor-car. As the war progressed design leapt ahead and more and more power was produced by both British and German engines.

The original rotaries gave 80 to 100 hp but the later BR1 Bentley rotary produced 150 hp and the later BR2 230 hp. This was the same W.O. Bentley who, after the war, found fame producing Bentley cars.

The French Nieuport 17s flown by Lionel Blaxland were powered by the 110 hp Le Rhône or the 130 hp Clerget rotaries. The earlier FE8s had also been powered by the same engines but the Albatros D2s that faced them had the water-cooled in-line 160 hp Mercedes engines and the later D3 had the higher compression version which produced more power.

The Sopwith Pups were fitted with various rotary engines; 80 hp Gnôme, 80 hp Clerget or 100 hp Gnômes. The first Sopwith Camels had 130 Clerget rotaries but 100 hp Gnômes and 110 hp Le Rhônes were also used. Some of the later Camels were fitted with the 150 hp Bentley BR1 and the last Sopwith fighter of the war, the Snipe, was designed to accept the latest 230 hp Bentley BR2 engine.

Above: Workmen at Packards prepare Liberty engines for final test in 1918. Packards produced Rolls-Royce Merlins in World War Two and Chris Harrison, the author's boss from Rolls-Royce days, was diverted from pilot training to help Packards build them. He went on to fly Mosquitos, some of them with Packard-built engines. *(US National Archive).*

Right: A German fitter installs a 160 hp Mercedes engine in an Albatros D3.

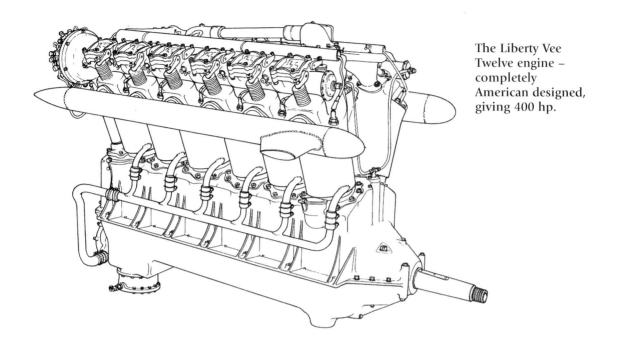

The Liberty Vee Twelve engine – completely American designed, giving 400 hp.

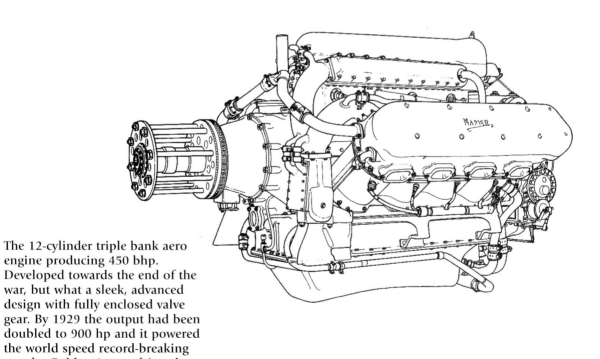

The 12-cylinder triple bank aero engine producing 450 bhp. Developed towards the end of the war, but what a sleek, advanced design with fully enclosed valve gear. By 1929 the output had been doubled to 900 hp and it powered the world speed record-breaking car, the Golden Arrow, driven by Sir Henry Seagrave who was a pilot in WWI.

As previously explained you could not call the water-cooled aero engines of the period beautiful, whether British or German: functional, yes, beautiful, no. The ugly exposed valve gear, reminiscent of a Christmas tree, certainly did nothing to help. There was, however, an exception: the Hispano Suiza designed by Marc Birkigd.

Birkigd was one of the greatest engineering designers of all time. Born in Geneva he was fascinated by electric power and went to Spain to work on electric locomotives but the new internal combustion engine soon fired his imagination and in 1904 he opened his Hispano Suiza factory with Spanish finance. In the next ten years he designed and produced 35 different models of motor cars culminating in the Alfonso XIII.

On the outbreak of World War One Spain remained neutral but Birkigd offered his services to France and created the Hispano vee eight water-cooled aero-engine that is still admired by engineers to this day.

Way ahead of its time it had an aluminium cylinder block with steel liners like the Rolls-Royce Merlin engines of World War Two. Valve operation was not the usual push rod overhead-valve but overhead camshaft and, unusually for the time, the valve gear was enclosed. The propeller was geared, not direct drive. This engine, too, merited the title twentieth century sculpture.

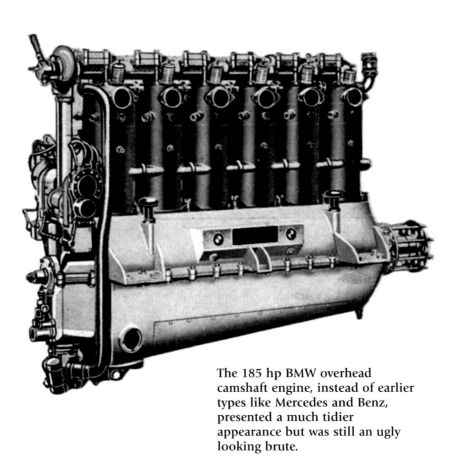

The 185 hp BMW overhead camshaft engine, instead of earlier types like Mercedes and Benz, presented a much tidier appearance but was still an ugly looking brute.

He made them in his factory and they were constructed under license in the US and England where they were later named the Wolesley Viper.

He also designed a mechanism to fire through the propeller shaft. No suitable machine tools were available so he designed and made them! Among the aircraft which used the Hispano were the Spad VII and the SE5a. The great French ace Guynemer in his Cigogne (Stork) Squadron successfully flew Hispano-powered machines and after the war Hispano adopted his squadron motif, the stork, for their cars.

Marc Birkigd was to continue making outstanding motor-cars. The Bristol Fighter was initially fitted with the water-cooled vee configuration Rolls-Royce 190 hp Falcon One and later the 220 hp Falcon Two. The plan was to fit the later models with 275 hp Falcon Threes but not enough were available so other makes were fitted with little success.

The Fokker Triplane originally used the 110 hp Oberursel and later the 145 hp version. Believe it or not the French 110 hp Le Rhônes were also used but built under license in Sweden. Other engines were also adopted experimentally.

The 1918 Fokker D7 was considered to be the best fighter of the war. It was fitted with the water-cooled in-line Mercedes engine or the 185 hp BMW.

The German version of rotary engine design. This is the 110 hp Oberursel.

The Bentley 200 hp BR2 Rotary.

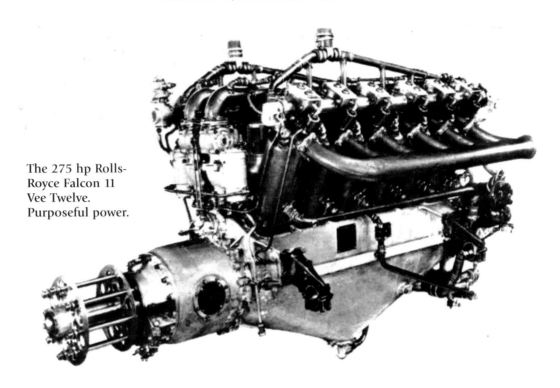

The 275 hp Rolls-Royce Falcon 11 Vee Twelve. Purposeful power.

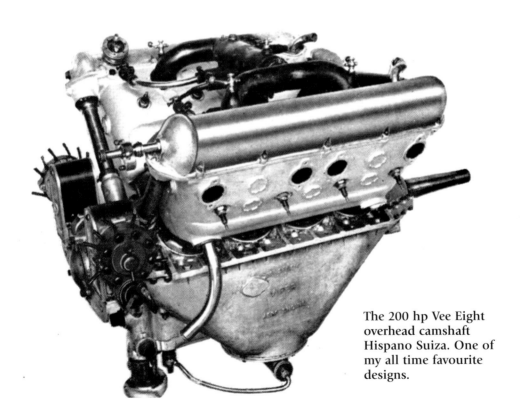

The 200 hp Vee Eight overhead camshaft Hispano Suiza. One of my all time favourite designs.

16

MCSCOTCH

Mannock christened William MacLanachan 'McScotch' and the later arrival George McElroy 'MacIrish'.

MacLanachan joined 40 Squadron in late May 1917 and survived against all the odds. He left in January 1918. In 1936 he wrote *Fighter Pilot* under the *nom-de-plume* McScotch and, like *An Airman's Wife*, his book gives us a fascinating account of his time in 40 Squadron. Fortunately he arrived when the Nieuports had replaced the FE8 deathtraps.

On his arrival Mannock took MacLanachan to see Lionel Blaxland. "So here you are," he said, "in Blaxland's hut." And to Lionel, "Here's your new mate, Blax. Look after him before he kills himself!"

From left to right, fighter pilots Rook, MacLanachan, Crole, Davies.

French 80 hp Caudron at Bruay. One that got away. What was it doing at Bruay? Note the peculiar biplane design! Huge top wing. Tiny bottom wing.

MacLanachan went on to write, "Blaxland was the one who had greeted me on arrival, a quiet, good-natured pilot, possibly two or three years older than myself." (Not so, Lionel was only nineteen years old) He went on to write: "His sedate manner created the impression of dignity beyond his years and the moderation of his opinions and his quiet voice inspired us with respect."

Dinner that evening was "a gloomy affair" but after dinner Mannock asked MacLanachan to join him in a walk down to the village. They chatted on the way there and back and established what was to develop into a long-term friendship.

In the village estaminet they had a drink together and chatted in broken English and French with Odette, the delightful seventeen-year-old French girl who served them.

MacLanachan and Lionel were woken next morning at 6am due to take off at 6.30. Lionel showed him a map of the front. (Many years later Lionel showed me this very same well-thumbed map but it had disappeared before Lionel's photograph albums and log book were passed on to John Simpkinson.)

Lionel pointed out the different landmarks: two pyramid-like dumps at Auchel, a peculiarly shaped wood behind Vimy and the two reservoirs behind the La Bassée canal. "These are the principal ones," said Lionel, "but when you get over the lines you will be able to make your own notes. We are about eleven miles from the front line now, just far enough to let us get a comfortable height before we cross."

MacLanachan went on to write:

> "Blaxland climbed steadily towards the east and in six or seven minutes we were flying over raw earthworks and trenches that stretched as far as the eye could see both to the north and to the south. The ground for miles on the east and west of these trenches was pock-marked with shell-holes amidst which we could discern the crumbling walls of shell-blasted houses. Except for one town, Lens, there was no sign of civilisation beneath us, but Lens, although the streets and houses were well defined, showed no signs of peaceful occupation, no smoke from the bare chimney stacks, no traffic in the streets... a deserted town just behind the German lines."

MacLanachan lost Lionel in a bank of cloud and when he did go down through the clouds again his landmarks had disappeared. He was not even sure which side of the lines he was on until he was encircled by the pungent black smoke of Archie bursts which made it clear that he was on the German side. Strangely enough he had made no mention of AA fire when crossing the lines.

Seeing a British FE2B he flew down towards it only to be amazed to see the observer standing up and aiming his machine-gun at him. He quickly realised that as he had approached out of the sun the observer had not been able to see the Nieuport clearly enough to recognise it as British. He quickly flew under the BE to enable the observer to see his RAF roundels. He then saw four machines approaching from the east but as he was unable to identify them he flew in the opposite direction. Finally, to his relief, he saw the Auchel dumps many miles away to the north west.

He landed at a British airfield to ask the way to Bruay and finally, after a two and three quarter hour flight arrived safely at Bruay to Lionel's great relief!

As MacLanachan had lost his leader this rather invalidated his first instructional flight so on the same afternoon Lionel took him up again and this time all went well.

In the evening he was posted to A Flight led by Captain Bath, an Australian. "If you lose the formation," he said, "it's quite easily done, fly west – but it's a line patrol and you should have the trenches to guide you." He was instructed to fly on the right hand extremity of a vee formation.

Fellow pilot Walder warned him that in the event of Huns diving on the formation he was to dive straight underneath the Nieuports as "we don't want them to get you!"

All his attention was concentrated on avoiding AA fire and keeping up with the flight. Next he saw Captain Bath waggle his wings… the signal for enemy in sight. The flight dived on a German green and yellow two-seater with the tracer bullets of the two leading machines clearly visible but he did not see the result.

Then flying carefully in formation and deciding that educational flights were over he was startled to hear the rat-tat-tat of a machine-gun behind him and saw tracer bullets whizzing by. A pointed-nose German plane dived past him but no sooner had it done so than the rat-tat-tat was repeated as another adversary dived on him and again a stream of tracers shot by.

Home safely at last with Captain Bath and Walder arguing about whether allowing a novice pilot to take up the rear position was dangerous to both him and the flight. Walder considered that it was.

Walder said to MacLanachan: "But why on earth didn't you dive as I told you to?" "I forgot," he replied, "and I was too interested in seeing what a German machine looked like anyway!" There were bullet holes in his right wing but beginner's luck had saved him. The experience, however, brought home to him that there was much to learn and that his education, far from being over, was only just beginning.

When MacLanachan joined the squadron the personnel had changed slightly. He wrote,

"It took me some time to get to know the other pilots and although there were only fourteen or fifteen of us several 'disappeared' before I even knew their names. Of the others Bond, Redler, Hall, Godfrey, Lever, Captain Allcock, Shaw, Parry, Captain Keen, Walder, Cudemore and New formed a hazy background to my first impression of the squadron. The friendliness of Mannock, Blaxland, Walder and Lewis helped me to get over the difficulties of the first few days and, with the mental stimulus obtained from my evening walks with Mannock, my attitude towards the 'War' underwent a change. The feeling of uncertainty and insecurity that had baulked me no longer persisted."

He explained that he had put in a good deal of effort, and no small amount of money in decorating the brown canvas Armstrong hut with blue cretonne. He and Blaxland lived in some comfort and "had it not been for the earwigs which abounded in the interior, we might have been considered 'civilised'". Reading his account of those first few weeks crossing the lines and facing AA fire and the enemy planes makes you realise how difficult it was for a newcomer to survive.

Mannock, believe it or not, rarely spoke of the actual fighting and "the only advice I got was from Lemon and Walder". The work of the squadron, he explained, was line patrols to prevent German aircraft crossing to our side of the lines, offensive patrols attacking German aircraft and balloons on the German side of the lines and escorts when they accompanied two-seater reconnaissance aircraft to protect them from attack while on bombing raids or photographic missions. He pointed out that you had to learn by experience and "in this haphazard schooling our knowledge of actual war fighting was tempered on the hard anvil of experience. We won each item of wisdom only at the risk of our lives. The fault did not lie so much in the actual flying training as in the lack of instruction in the 'psychology of fighting'. Nothing had been done to 'key' me up to the dangers that assailed us – it was a question of learn or die."

Captain Bath asked him to look after a new pilot on his first patrol. Crossing the lines they were met by the usual AA barrage but instead of keeping to his orders the new pilot took up a parallel course about half a mile away from the flight.

MacLanachan flew towards him in an attempt to get him back but he simply flew further away. The new pilot then returned to his position half a mile away from the flight.

He was, of course, as a lone flyer at great risk of being picked off by enemy fighters. On their return Captain Bath and the other pilots had been equally concerned about the tyro's behaviour but when questioned he said that as the flight seemed to relish being where the shells were exploding he did not see why he should be compelled to do so. Although they tried to explain how vulnerable he was to attack by abandoning the flight in this manner and that for his own safety he should stay with the flight, nothing they could say made any impression on him.

During the next flight he remained outside as before and "we saw him no more". No one regretted his going, for "in our vernacular he asked for it and got it".

During his first two weeks there were a number of departures and arrivals. Several pilots went missing, others posted to Home Establishment after having served six months with the squadron.

The British attack on Vimy Ridge had meant heavy casualties in the RFC leaving the pilots who had survived exhausted and nerve racked. The lucky pilots sent home acted as instructors or on home defence when, after three or four months, they would return to France to fight again.

MacLanachan's views on flying the Nieuport are of interest: His machine-gun was left as supplied by the factory and fired 15 degrees above the line of flight. This meant that a pilot had to dive to attack at a steeper angle than a pilot with his gun firing along the line of flight.

He also recognised that the Albatri and Halberstadts were significantly faster and their pilots could choose to outrun the Nieuports any time they wished.

He also commented ruefully on the far superior firepower of the Germans' twin Spandaus. Like so many other British pilots he pointed out what a disadvantage it was to have to cope with the prevailing south-westerly winds. A tremendous disadvantage pushing against the wind on the way back especially if in difficulties due to wounds, a damaged machine or an engine failure. It also meant that their reduced speed fighting against the wind made the German AA gunners' task considerably easier.

About a fortnight after his first flight over the lines a German two-seater in yellow and green had been attacked by the patrol on two consecutive evenings. On the third evening MacLanachan decided to have a go on his own. He did, indeed, encounter the yellow and green two-seater about 2,000 ft below him so with murder in mind he dived onto it.

He approached to within certain killing range and with his eye pressed to the Aldis sight he pressed the firing lever. Nothing happened. In his excitement he had forgotten to cock the gun. So close then that he had to pull out of the dive.

Two wires hung down from the gun: One to cock it and the other to release it so that it could be pulled down for reloading. He pulled the cocking lever but by mistake, it was the release lever and the gun fell down hitting him a stunning blow on the head.

Temporarily blinded and almost senseless he heard, to his horror, the rat-tat-tat of machine-gun fire. He was being attacked by six or seven enemy machines… the yellow and green two-seater had been a trap!

For a novice to get out of such a situation required a miracle…. but the miracle was granted. Diving, spinning, twisting, turning, sideslipping with a cloud of smoke streamers from German incendiary bullets surrounding his machine he avoided almost certain death while the Germans attacked him "with all the vigour of a pack of hounds after a defenceless stag".

Somehow he managed to reload his gun while in a plummeting spiral but then the German AA fire opened up with a vengeance. Twenty or so nerve-shattering detonations appeared in

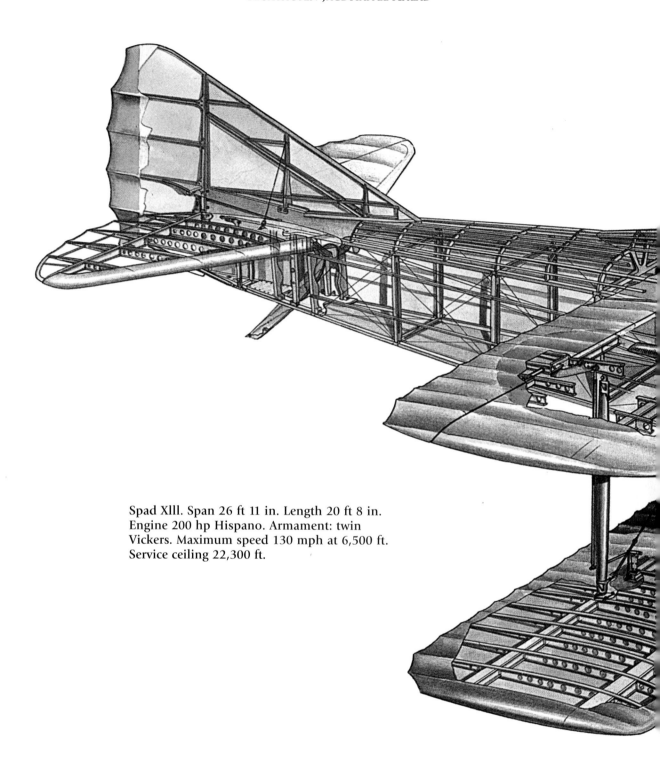

Spad Xlll. Span 26 ft 11 in. Length 20 ft 8 in.
Engine 200 hp Hispano. Armament: twin
Vickers. Maximum speed 130 mph at 6,500 ft.
Service ceiling 22,300 ft.

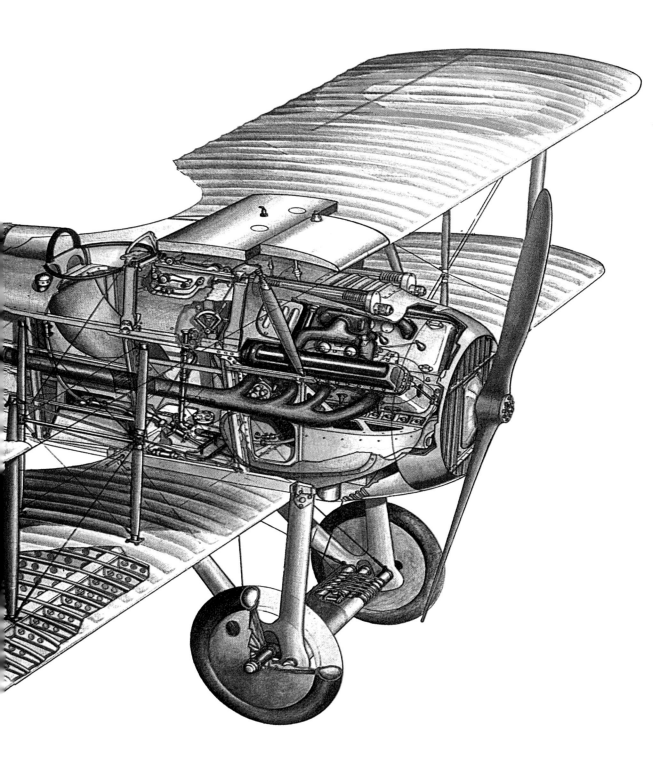

front of the Nieuport but, somehow, the machine survived and at last he was over the lines and back towards home.

But important lessons had been learned and he had lived to fight another day. Firstly the two-seater had already been attacked at the same time on two consecutive days so the third time was almost certainly a trap. Secondly never again confuse the Lewis gun release lever with the cocking wire.

He went over the lines again next day at 16,000 feet and encountered two enemy machines ten miles or so on the other side of the lines. Both turned and fired at him but without effect. He fired at one only 100 yards away and saw the bullets strike into the fuselage just behind the engine and the machine went into a steep dive. The other machine flew off. Again severe anti-aircraft fire had to be endured as he re-crossed the lines but he got home safely.

On his return Major Tilney pointed out that only pilots with a roving commission were allowed to fly solo on the other side of the lines and, in any case, as there was no supporting evidence of his claim it could not be allowed.

"How I envied fighters like Bond, Blaxland, Walder, Hall, Lemon, Keen and Redler," he wrote. "Both Bond and Godfrey had succeeded in bringing down two enemy machines in one day. They were my idols during those first weeks."

During his first fortnight with the squadron his chief interest was to learn the habits of the 'line' and have many discussions with Mannock who was off flying for seven days due to getting a small piece of steel in his eye.

In the middle of June two fellow pilots who learned to fly with him were posted to the squadron. G.B. Crole and Peter Wylie Smith, an Australian. Crole was a fellow Scot and a double Oxford Blue. He was a former observer and quickly fitted in but his introduction to the Nieuport was none too promising. The machine he was first given required full left rudder as it came in to land and you had to "kick the rudder hard over". But, despite MacLanachan's warning he failed to do this and on touching the ground the machine cartwheeled over.

Crole was dragged out of the wreck badly shaken and with a bruised leg but despite this he went up in another machine and this time made a perfect landing.

Peter Wylie, however, "Never quite succeeded in mastering the Nieuport. His landings were OK but in the air the idiosyncrasies of the machine caused him endless trouble; so much so that, despite his willingness to go on trying and his undoubted courage, Major Tilney was forced to send him to Candas for 'further instruction'. Fortunately, after a fortnight's instruction, he was able to return to the squadron."

MacLanachan persevered with his flying education and when not on official patrol he went up and down the lines to gain yet more experience. On one of these trips he was crossing the lines and saw a black and red Albatros two-seater 1,500 ft or so below him. At point-blank range he fired twenty rounds into it and "it put its nose up into the air, rearing like a wounded animal", before falling over and plunging earthwards with flames licking round the fuselage.

It was the first time that he had seen a machine falling in flames and he was "horrified and soul sickened". It was, however, his first official victory. He was later to see a number of his own and German pilots plummet down in flames but always with a silent prayer, hoping that the pilot, British or German, had been killed first.

Many pilots crashed on returning from patrol due to a number of causes: tyres punctured by bullets or AA fragments, engine failure, structural damage, wounds, for example.

One Sunday morning returning from patrol he heard a grinding noise and then...nothing. Until he woke up in hospital.

It appeared that he had crashed into another machine.

An infantry attack soon filled the hospital beds and although far from fit he discharged himself and returned to the squadron.

Back in the squadron with nerves still shaky, Major Tilney allowed him to borrow a motorcycle and sidecar as soon as he was fit enough, to visit friends in the area and adjoining squadrons.

Nearest was 2 Squadron at Hesdigneux on the Béthune road. They flew Armstrong-Whitworth two-seaters whose principal task was artillery spotting, flying at the dangerously low altitude of 2,000 – 4,000 ft. In addition they flew low-level bombing attacks on railheads and supply columns.

Another of their tasks was photographic reconnaissance. MacLanachan wrote: "We frequently saw them miles on the German side of the line, surrounded by clouds of Archie bursts, plodding at their disagreeable tasks." 40 Squadron often provided them with fighter escort to protect them from enemy fighters.

At Auchel, only three miles away, Squadrons 25 and 43 shared the airfield. No. 25 was a bomber squadron flying the pusher FE2Ds with the observer in front of the pilot and able to fire forwards and upwards. At night they would often be heard flying over Bruay to bomb German aerodromes and towns.

Another nearby squadron was the redoubtable Naval 8, at Mount Eloi. At that time it was flying Sopwith Triplanes and their patrols co-operated with No. 40. They later changed to Sopwith Camels and were commanded by the inimitable 'Mad Major' Draper, but more of him later.

The 'Tripes' were both faster and more manoeuvrable than the Nieuports. Their aerodrome was shared by 16 Squadron, a Canadian Squadron flying the two-seater RE8s...Harry Tates! They specialised in artillery co-operation and 40 Squadron pilots frequently saw them evading AA fire while sending back their wireless messages to British batteries. Their pilots took a pride in never giving way to German fighters unless hopelessly outnumbered and by staying in fights they often brought down enemy fighters.

Although fighting in the air was a serious and desperate business there were lighter moments, too. Tennis, cards, music on the gramophone, discussions on everything from the war to cabbages and kings. Excellent dinners in the mess followed by after dinner speeches, controversial debates, then music on the piano of ill omen or Mick Mannock's violin. Tea at Odettes or at the Queen of Sheba's at Béthune or in a cellar of the almost totally obliterated town of Bully-Grenay. Dinners at Béthune, Amiens or, occasionally, St. Omer.

But despite these pleasures the fighter pilot's expectation of life was "journalistically computed at *three weeks*!"

The *dramatis personae* of the squadron continued to change as pilots were shot down, sent on leave or on Home Defence or invalided out. Davis was a popular newcomer in A Flight, getting away to a splendid start. Another new flight commander was the South African 'Zulu' Lloyd. Other South Africans were Hall, Redler and Tudhope. Tudhope's cheery personality

Sopwith Pup & Clouds by PWP (*Captain Collet*).

granted him instant acceptance.

Lionel left the squadron on July 12th 1917 to go onto Home Defence but during July there was, surprisingly, an undercurrent of dissention against Mannock.

Mannock had gained in confidence since first joining the squadron. He was no longer silent when others talked and his sense of social inferiority had vanished but he now had to face another kind of snobbery – his fighting prowess.

He had been with the squadron for two months and had only brought down two enemy machines. Some pilots considered that he had deliberately avoided combat when others went into a fight. They also resented the development of Mick Mannock's self-assurance. But this was unjust: his self confidence was the result of his experience and acceptance.

The squadron showed no mercy to 'quitters', it's true, but even to suspect that Mannock could possibly be a quitter was manifestly unfair.

On one occasion with Captain Bath leading the flight they dived onto seven or eight German planes near Henin-Liétard. A fierce dogfight ensued with "the air filled with stunting, scrapping machines. Here and there were the flashes of British tracer bullets or the smoke trails of the Germans'."

MacLanachan got his sights on an enemy but his gun stopped firing. After two rounds…his firing pin had broken.

So there he was unarmed in the middle of a dogfight. Nothing for it but to spin down out of the fight and head for home at the mercy of his opponents.

When the rest of the pilots arrived it looked as if he had abandoned them in the middle of a fight until the broken bolt acquitted him, and he was stoutly defended by Mannock.

More new pilots had arrived – Crole, Tudhope, Pettigrew, Kennedy, Rook, Peter. W. Smith, Harrison……

Harrison and Kennedy, both Canadians, were posted to A Flight. Harrison was an odd ball. Six feet tall, bristly hair and quarrelsome. He had his own views about the war and the flight. He neither smoked nor drank.

MacLanachan took him for his first instructional flight over the lines. He had never flown in formation or even had any idea of flying in a straight line. MacLanachan told him to fly as close to him as possible but 'Harrie' failed to "control either his forward speed or direction. He would appear for a few seconds to my right then, after getting behind me, would come up on my left in a series of jerks and sideslips."

Back at the aerodrome Harrie was not merely unrepentant but furious.

"Of all the bloody fool pilots I've met," he said addressing Captain Bath, "This fellow takes the xyz cake!"

MacLanachan could well have been blamed for not taking care of a novice pilot on his first patrol with the flight. They did not have to look for trouble but "Harrie provided plenty of it".

"Harrie's Nieuport seemed to bear a grudge against all the others; it would come charging sideways towards us and, on our frantic efforts to avoid a collision, we would be greeted by the sight of Harrie careering off in an equally desperate sideslip towards the next machine."

Back at the aerodrome Captain Bath told Harrie exactly what he thought of his performance but it cut no ice with Harrie. "None of you xyz's can fly straight. I'll get the CO to put me in another flight."

Fortunately Harrie did eventually learn to fly and despite his "aggressively taciturn manner" became an accepted member of the squadron.

Harrie's fellow Canadian, Kennedy, was an entirely different character. Twenty-one years old he had attended Toronto University. His particularly keen sense of humour quickly endeared him to the squadron.

Both Harrie and Kennedy were keen poker players and poker became all the rage. A game between Steve Godfrey, Harrie, George Pettigrew, Kennedy and Hall was always fascinating. The inscrutable Harrie only occasionally bluffed, Steve was always ready to "put the other fellow up" and George always did his best to raise the pitch of the game.

Rook was a Canadian, aged nineteen the same age as Barlow, the "babies" of the squadron with much in common and both of them always ready for a 'rag'. Rook regarded the war with due seriousness while Barlow treated it as if it was really a rag on a stupendous scale.

One of the Naval 8 pilots carried out a one-man raid on a German aerodrome so Barlow decided to do the same. He returned "almost speechless with excitement, claiming to have shot down a German plane but had been riddled by bullets from the air and the ground on the way back but, of course, with no witnesses the German plane could not be confirmed."

After trying unsuccessfully to intercept a two-seater that had the temerity to fly across the lines, Mannock finally managed it and sent it crashing down into the British trenches near Avion. Mannock was "flushed with excitement while waiting for a tender to take him to the crashed machine but his mood changed abruptly when he got up to it." The plane was a DFW and it had crashed into what had been former German trenches before the battle of Arras. The pilot was dead and the observer, a captain, was wounded. The pilot's dog was dead beside him and the pilot's body was just blood and bones.

This sickened Mannock but, as he explained to MacLanachan, he had missed so many enemy machines that he had begun to think that he could not see a target correctly. "No matter how much nausea it causes," he said, "I had to find out and this one down on our side was my chance."

Not only did the sight of the dead pilot upset him but the journey up to the wreck was a shocking experience. In their hurried advance the Canadians had no time to bury the dead and the sights and stench were shocking. MacLanachan accompanied Mannock on the same journey a day or two later.

Decomposing arms and legs were sticking out of the clay, some with sleeves and puttees, others just bare bones. "Half buried in the mud of a trench was a skull from which the flesh had been gnawed by the army of grey shapes that slunk away from us into the dugouts, over it all hung the overpowering, sickening stench of death."

Mannock and MacLanachan were furious that the observer had been a captain but the pilot merely an NCO.

During the next few weeks the squadron was constantly engaged in aerial fighting and on one day they were to claim a bag of four enemy machines.

"The old scrappers like Steve Godfrey, Mick, Zulu Lloyd, Hall, Blaxland, Keen and Redler continued their destructive work… while the more junior members Crole, Pettigrew, Kennedy, Rook and Barlow each accounted for several enemy machines."

MacLanachan heard the details of Crole's first victory from Blaxland. They had encountered

Captain Stroud. SE 5as arrived at 40 Squadron after Lionel left for home defence, but he did fly them in England.

four Albatri near Douai and Crole had fired at one at point-blank range to see it break up in the air and plunge down in flames.

The Bruay aerodrome was eleven miles from the lines so the squadron was supplied with a forward landing ground only one and half miles from the trenches. It was also shared by 43 Squadron.

40 called it Mazingarbe. 43 called it Petit Saints after the farm on which it was situated. Only rudimentary facilities were provided.

It was useful also for signalling to British pilots if any machines were nearby. Although close to the lines it was seldom troubled by German artillery though nearby Bully-Grenay was continually shelled even though it was merely a skeleton village where all the houses had been destroyed.

Even so, the philosophic farmer at Petit Saints still continued with his usual work of ploughing and sowing or growing clover where ploughing was impossible.

Mannock, Keen, Godfrey and Zulu Lloyd spent much of their days over the lines looking for prey. MacLanachan. too, followed suit.

About this time Blaxland's and Walder's tours of duty ended and Lionel was sent to Home Establishment. Captain Bath fell ill and went into hospital. He was replaced by Bill Bond but while he was on leave Redler took over.

Corporal Godfrey from the orderly room was asking for Mr Mannock: he held a telegram saying that 2nd Lieutenant Mannock had been awarded the Military Cross. This stiffened Mannock's resolve even more firmly to knock down those Huns.

On July 21st MacLanachan was on an A Flight patrol led by Bill Bond. They saw two machines going down in flames. Arriving back at the aerodrome they found that one of them was a plane from 43 Squadron and the other one was Rook. A severe blow to the squadron.

There was a superstition in the squadron that whoever played the battered piano in the mess would not live longer than a week. Hall, Steve Godfrey and Redler claimed that they knew a number of instances in which this had happened. Rook had played the piano less than a week before his death.

On July 22nd Bill Bond made his last flight and MacLanachan witnessed his death, as described in an earlier chapter.

Mick Mannock was then promoted to be in charge of A Flight; a move that was not welcomed by all pilots. Somehow he had not yet lived down his reputation of being "slightly yellow"… he was "soft" and pandered to the CO… he was a lone fighter who could only lose his head with success. Mannock, however, wrote in his letter to his friends the Eyles on the day of his award "Secret! Got the MC, old boy, and made Captain and Flight Commander on probation. Don't tell anyone and still write to me as the usual Lieutenant."

Before a week was out Mannock had proved his courage and ability beyond all doubt.

17

MANNOCK'S FINAL DAYS IN FRANCE

Redler had spent over six months with the squadron and then the doctor found out that he had been suffering from a complaint that several had tried to conceal, bleeding at the nose. He was sent home for a rest as an instructor in a training squadron.

Tudhope was transferred to A Flight, Mannock went from strength to strength. Mannock, Tudhope, MacLanachan, Kennedy, Harrison, Zulu Lloyd, Godfrey, Crole, Keen… all pushed hard to keep the sky clear of German aircraft, often using Mazingarbe as a rendezvous.

MacLanachan changed to a newer Nieuport 24 with a circular fuselage unlike the box section fuselage of the Nieuport 17. Faster, too, than the 17 with a more powerful engine and with twin Lewis guns on the top plane which delighted him.

Mannock, Tudhope and Kennedy decided to strafe a German aerodrome but endured a tremendous pasting. They all got back but Tudhope's machine's top plane had been shot to ribbons, all his instruments were smashed and a bullet had passed through his coat collar.

"I've had all the gruelling I want this morning, " said Mannock, "my God, never had such a wind-up in my life."

Air fighting intensified from the end of July to the beginning of August with more German planes in the air, though still staying on their side of the lines.

Balloon busting continued – always a dangerous business – and on occasion all the planes returned spattered with bullet holes. On one occasion Mannock's plane was so badly shot-up that it was a write-off. Trench strafing was another dangerous task.

At Mazingarbe one evening Kennedy confessed a premonition to MacLanachan. Only twenty-one years old he said he would never get home to see his fiancée again. MacLanachan did his best to dismiss this premonition as nonsense but a few days later on patrol MacLanachan saw an Albatros going down in an uncontrolled spin and shortly afterwards a Nieuport. It was Kennedy's so his premonition was proved correct.

Kennedy's place was filled by a new pilot, McElroy, who, as stated above, was christened 'MacIrish' by Mannock to distinguish between the two Macs in his flight.

Although McElroy initially had no success with the Nieuports he showed his true worth when 40 Squadron later changed to SE5s and went on to be one of the leading aces of the war. More of this later.

Mannock on a borrowed motorcycle visited nearby AA units to help improve their chances of bringing down enemy machines and MacLanachan did the same.

Mannock was a talented violinist and often played in the mess after dinner but Rook and Kennedy's deaths put everyone off playing that accursed piano!

On September 14th Mannock was awarded a bar to his MC. He had grown more and more confident and become a much more rounded and likeable character. The taciturn Harrie had mellowed, too, and became part of the A Flight family though he had not yet managed to score a victory.

Of this period MacLanachan wrote:

> "At any one period there were always six or seven pilots in the squadron who had reached the stage of development (efficient fighter but also capable of keeping clear of enemy bullets) which, unfortunately, only lasted three or four months. Nerves and health could not stand the strain much longer than that and it was then that pilots were returned to Home Establishment for a rest."

Hall and Godfrey were sent back in mid-September and Crole was given command of a flight in 43 Squadron which was being equipped with Sopwith Camels.

Peter Smith never managed to master the Nieuport's propensity to spin yet, somehow, was always able to pull out and survive until finally his luck ran out and he spun from 10,000 feet right into the ground. Almost every bone in his body was broken, one eye was missing and his thumb torn off… but, incredibly, he survived and, even more incredibly, he was flying again within a year.

Newcomer, Nutter, crashed his machine into the aerodrome and was killed. Barlow was killed before the end of September, shot down on the British side of the lines. MacLanachan wanted to see the body and pay his last respects but Major Tilney advised him not to. "It would make too much impression on you, he's terribly smashed up."

Mannock started to take his patrol higher and higher right up to 20,000 feet on MacLanachan's altimeter, the uppermost limit of the Nieuport's performance where MacLanachan experienced "a bitter bone-striking cold". Back from patrol Mick commented on his machine's tendency to fall out of his hands at 15,000 feet only to be told by Tudhope and Harrison that it was 22,000 feet on their altimeters. Mick's altimeter had stuck at 15,000 feet!

Finally in December 1917 SE5as replaced the outclassed Nieuports. 56 Squadron had leapt ahead with these new planes which were so much faster, and better armed, than the Nieuports: 120 mph in level flight and 200 mph in a dive, against the Nieuport's 150 mph.

They still had a Lewis gun on the top plane but also had a Vickers gun firing through the propeller. I have never understood why twin Vickers were never used on the SEs as they had already been successfully used on Sopwith Camels.

But contrary to 56's experience, 40 Squadron got off to a very bad start with the new machines. The engines supplied to 40 Squadron were hopelessly unreliable and within a fortnight the squadron experienced twenty engine failures. MacLanachan had four in a week. Mannock was furious.

The Vickers guns frequently jammed and, even worse, the Constanesco interrupter gear was not installed correctly so that many propellers were damaged by bullets. For three weeks the squadron failed to bag a single enemy machine.

Such was General Trenchard's concern that he visited 40 Squadron to hear their complaints and, as a result, the Headquarters gunnery officer was sent over. Eventually engine and armament problems were sorted out and pilots who had never managed to achieve success in Nieuports found their form in the SEs.

By the end of December Mannock's nerves were at twanging point after such a long spell at the front but, fortunately, both he and MacLanachan were sent home in early January 1918. MacLanachan never returned to France and this undoubtedly saved his life.

After a time in England Mannock returned to even greater success in 74 Squadron where he finally met his death. He went back to France at the end of March 1918 as a flight commander in the newly formed 74 Squadron. In the next three months he added another 36 to his score to make 59 but the consensus of opinion (despite Douglass Whetton's view) was that his true total was at the very least four more.

He was awarded a DSO in May 1918 with a bar two weeks later. He left the squadron to go on leave in June returning to France in July to command 85 Squadron. During his leave he spent some time with Jimmy McCudden but on July 9th Jimmy's death dealt him a tremendous blow; even so, however, he returned to combat with renewed vigour.

Newcomer to the squadron, young Donald Inglis, had not yet managed to score a victory. "Have you got a Hun yet, Inglis?" asked Mannock. "No, Sir," he replied. "Well come on out and we will get one," said Mannock.

Inglis's plane, however, could not take off due to a jammed elevator wheel but next morning they both set out as dawn was breaking. Donald Inglis later described the flight as follows:

> "My instructions were to sit on Mick's tail, and that he would waggle his wings if he wanted me closer. I soon found that I didn't have much chance of looking round, as Mick would waggle, and the only thing I could do was to watch his tail and sit tight, as he was flying along the lines at about thirty to fifty feet up and not straight for more than a few seconds, first up on one wing tip, then the other. Suddenly he turned towards home full out and climbing. "A Hun" thought I, but I'm damned if I could find one; then a quick turn and a dive, and there was Mick shooting up a Hun two-seater. He must have got the observer, as when he pulled up and I came in underneath him I didn't see the Hun shooting. I flushed the Hun's petrol tank and just missed ramming his tail as it came up when the Hun's nose dropped. Falling in behind Mick again we did a couple of circles round the burning wreck and then made for home. I then saw Mick start to kick his rudder and realised we were fairly low, then I saw a flame come out of the side of his machine; it grew bigger and bigger. Mick was no longer kicking his rudder, his nose dropped slightly and he went into a slow right-hand turn round about twice, and hit the ground in a burst of flame. I circled at about twenty feet but could not see him, and as things were getting pretty hot, made for home and managed to reach our outposts with a punctured petrol tank. Poor old Mick. All that I could say when I got into the trench was that the bloody buggers had shot

my Major down in flames."

So the greatest British air fighter of the war was killed, not in combat with an enemy machine but by a bullet from the ground.

But why did he fly so close to the ground? Something that all his experience would have told him not to do. Surely it must be put down to war weariness. Did he manage to reach for his revolver before the flames engulfed him? We will never know.

Strangely enough his arch-enemy, Manfred von Richthofen, made the same mistake and he, too, paid for it with his life. War weariness again?

18

RICHTHOFEN – THE RED BARON

The Red Baron or, to give him his full name, Manfred Freiherr von Richthofen, is surely the most famous name in WW1 aviation. He was the highest scoring pilot of them all with eighty victories. An enormous amount has been written about him but, even so, I must devote a chapter to him in this book.

He came from a Prussian military family whose tradition was that the eldest son should join the army. Manfred was to follow this tradition.

The eldest son, he was born in 1892. Second son Lothar (pronounced Lo-tar) followed in 1894, also destined to become an ace. Youngest son Bolko was born in 1903 so was too young to serve in the war. Manfred joined the army as a cadet and became a cavalry officer in an Ulan Regiment. He was a fearless rider and brilliant rifle shot.

In 1914 he encountered the enemy and realised that the role of the cavalry in modern war was over. He was transferred to the infantry and finally his repeated attempts to get into the flying service were successful in May 1915.

His first flying was as an observer in a two-seater on the Russian Front where he met Oswald Boelcke who was there on a visit. At that time Boelcke was making his name flying the unbeatable Fokker Eindekker (monoplane) on the Western Front in France. Richthofen asked Boelcke the secret of his success: "Fly close to your adversary, aim carefully....and fire." replied Boelcke: a simple enough instruction that Richthofen was later to put into deadly effect.

He was determined to become a pilot and finally succeeded after twenty training flights. He flew as the pilot of a two-seater C Class Albatros at Verdun and shot down a French Nieuport but it fell within French territory and there were no witnesses to confirm it. Strangely enough all Richthofen's official victories were against British machines.

Back to the Russian Front in two-seaters again but this time as a pilot. Serving at Kovel flying on light bombing raids he was again visited by Boelcke who was looking for promising pilots to fly in France: Richthofen was chosen. As he left a fellow pilot shouted: "Don't come back without the *Pour Le Merite*!" If only he had known what the future would bring.

Richthofen was in luck. The new Albatros D2 biplanes had arrived with their deadly twin Spandaus and on September 17th 1916 he scored his first victory, shooting down a two-seater FE2b from 11 Squadron. All the other pilots who flew with him that day scored too, as did Boelcke.

Fokker DR1 Triplane. Span 23 ft 7 in. Length 19 ft. Engine 110 hp
Oberursel. Armament: twin Spandaus. Maximum speed 115 mph
ground level. Service ceiling 19, 600 ft.

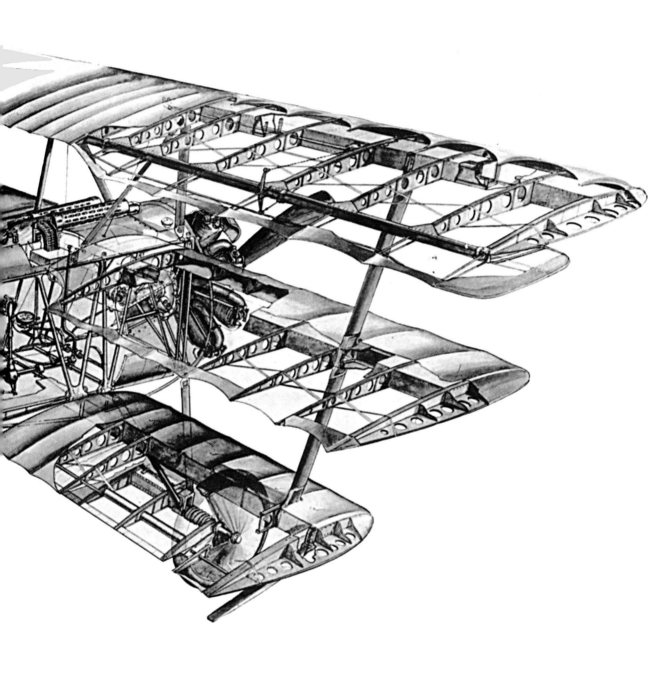

Manfred von Richthofen (centre) with his Jasta 11 pilots. Vizefeldwebel Sebastian Festner (12 victories), Leutnant Karl Schaffer (30), Oberleutnant Lothar von Richthofen (40), Oberleutnant Kurt Wolff (33). *(Imperial War Museum)*

By November 9th he had already recorded eight victories and on the 23rd he shot down the celebrated Major Lanoe Hawker, flying a DH2.

After his 16th victory he was given command of Jasta 11 and two days later was awarded the *Pour le Merite.*

After his 18th victory on January 24th the upper wing of his Albatros D3 broke off in the air but, even so, he landed safely. On the same day Jasta Boelcke lost three Albatri; could it have been due to the same cause?

On March 9th 1917 came the epic battle with 40 Squadron as described in the opening chapter. On April 2nd he shot down an aircraft in the morning and another in the afternoon for his thirty-ninth victory.

The Richthofen Circus was formed at the end of June, the most formidable flying, fighting combination of the war. Richthofen had four units under his command; commanding Jasta 4 was Oberleutnant Von Doering who in the Second World War became fighter leader on the Russian Front.

Leutnant Karl Allmenröder's Albatros D3 after Jasta 11's move to Roucourt. The aircraft appears to be all red but for white nose and spinner.

Leading Jasta 6 was Oberleutnant Dostler, already credited with 15 victories. Jasta 10 was led by Oberleutnant Freiherr Von Althaus but soon succeeded by Werner Voss. Jasta 11 by the brilliant Leutnant Wolff, already with thirty victories to his credit.

The average age of the leaders was twenty-five and the pilots twenty-one. Soon afterwards Richthofen was wounded in combat and had to spend three weeks in hospital. He eventually changed from Albatros machines to a nimble Fokker Triplane and his successes continued.

He finally met his death on April 21st 1918 and his score of eighty victories was never to be surpassed.

But the manner of his death was at variance with the principles of air fighting that he had always followed. Most of his victories were over German-held territory. When he did venture over the British lines it was high in the air to avoid ground fire, yet on his last flight he was down to tree-top height in combat with Sopwith Camels.

Overleaf: **This was Richthofen's last flight on April 21st 1918. Richthofen was low down in the Somme valley pursuing novice pilot 'Wop' May's Sopwith Camel. Roy Brown, a fellow Canadian and May's former school friend, also flying a Camel, was on Richthofen's tail and credited, at the time, with shooting him down. Now, however, following extensive research, it seems certain he was shot down by ground fire. This painting was commissioned for the book by the author from John Batchelor.**

So was it war weariness that condemned him to a death like Mick Mannock's? This surely must be the case. He was pursuing a Sopwith Camel with another Camel piloted by Roy Brown on his tail.

On April 21st Canadian Captain A.R Brown of 209 Squadron headed out on patrol in his Sopwith Camel accompanied by Lieutenants Lomas, Mackenzie and Second Lieutenant W.R. May. May was a fellow Canadian and a school friend of Roy Brown. This was his first offensive patrol and Roy Brown had told him to stay high and avoid any combat.

Richthofen's flight saw two RE8s on the British side of the lines and attacked them. Roy Brown saw this and headed to attack joined by another flight of Camels from 205 Squadron.

In the following dogfight Camels and Triplanes whirled round getting lower and lower. Unable to resist the challenge and ignoring his instructions, May joined the scrap. Eventually at very low altitude May found a Triplane on his tail firing bursts at him before it was lost out of sight. He said that the Triplane pilot turned round at the moment he fired but whether it was merely a backward glance or the involuntary reflex of a man who had been hit is hard to judge.

Brown was certain that he had shot the Triplane down and was credited with the victory but eyewitnesses on the ground were equally certain that the Triplane was brought down by machine-gun fire from the ground.

May and Richthofen were both flying at tree-top level and several ground-based machine-guns had fired at the Triplane. It appears that an Australian machine-gunner named Popkin has the strongest claim but, even today, there is no absolute certainty as to who shot Richthofen down.

So, as in Mannock's case, Richthofen also met his death when flying close to the ground over enemy territory. Something that neither of them would ever have done in their earlier days.

19

THE GREATER FIGHTER PILOT: RICHTHOFEN OR MANNOCK?

This is a question that has been endlessly debated. Richthofen scored more victories than anyone else; a total of eighty. Other pilots had the same opportunities but were never able to match his score.

Mannock, however, was behind Richthofen with arguably seventy-three victories but did this make him the lesser fighter pilot? I don't think so and here is the evidence.

Richthofen was not afraid to attack any opponent, either single-seater fighter or two-seater reconnaissance plane but his earlier victories were against far inferior opponents, mostly two-seater reconnaissance planes. His machines outperformed and outgunned his adversaries so he got off to a tremendous start when so many planes were 'easy meat'.

Mannock, by comparison, initially flew Nieuport 17s which were inferior in performance to the German Albatros D2s and D3s. In addition the Nieuports were handicapped by a single Lewis gun on the top plane, with far inferior firepower.

When Mannock did finally move onto SE5as he had, at last, the advantage of a single synchronised Vickers gun firing through the propeller but he still had that ridiculous Lewis gun on the top plane.

So Mannock never did fly a machine on equal terms with the fighter opposition but, even so, achieved only slightly fewer victories. In addition to this Mannock was known to have credited others with victories that he could rightly have claimed himself.

Surely, then, on level terms and given the same opponents that Richthofen had faced in 1916 Mannock's score would have eclipsed that of Richthofen.

The Fokker Triplane DR1 425/17 in which Richthofen ostensibly scored his last two victories. Dark red on all upper surfaces with a white rudder, the original Maltese Cross was overpainted into the Greek Cross design.

Captain Roy Brown of 209 Squadron RAF with his Sopwith Camel B7270 in which he flew when pursuing Richthofen on April 21st 1918.

Avro 504 two-seater. Span 36 ft length 29 ft 5 in. Engine 110 hp Le Rhône. Armament: one Lewis. Maximum speed 95 mph at ground level, service ceiling 18,000 ft. Several variants. This is the later 504K. The first organised bombing raid in history was made by four 504s attacking the Zeppelin sheds at Friedrichschafen on November 21st 1914. Relegated to training duties by mid 1915.

Avro 504 (100 hp Mono).

Avro. This pupil would appear to require further instruction!

Nose of an Avro.

RE7 140 RAF.

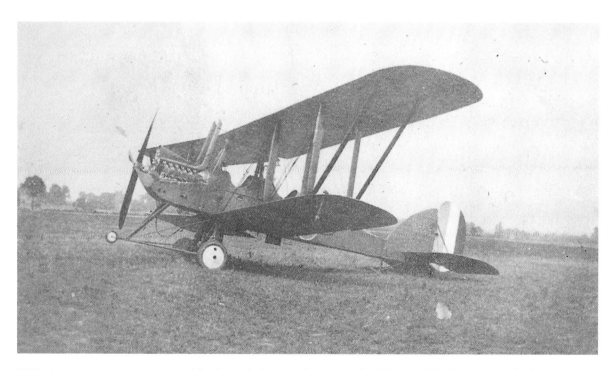

RE7. A rare two-seater snapped by Lionel. It came between the RE5 and the later RE8 which was flown by 17 British squadrons. I know very little about the RE7, but understand that it was powered by the 150 hp RAF engine.

Some of the pilots. No caption by Lionel, so who were they?

20

GEORGE EDWARD HENRY McELROY

McElroy was probably the most successful Irish fighter pilot of the Great War. He was born at Donnybrook near Dublin in 1893. On leaving school he entered the Civil Service but volunteered as a dispatch rider on the outbreak of war. He crossed to France in October 1914 and in May 1915 was commissioned into the Royal Irish Regiment only to be badly gassed shortly afterwards and returned to the UK.

Fit again he fought in Ireland in the Easter Rebellion, April 1916. After a spell in the Royal Garrison Artillery he enlisted in the RFC in April 1917.

In August 1917 he joined 40 Squadron at Bruay, then flying Nieuport 17s but he had no success with them, nor did he ever feel comfortable in them. The change to SE5s however, transformed his fortunes and he was, at last, in a machine that suited him perfectly. Despite the unreliability of 40 Squadron's engines and machine-guns, he scored his first victory on December 28th 1917.

From then on he was unstoppable and went on to become one of the most successful air fighters of the war. He was an outstanding shot, scoring many victories at long range and, in addition, with an incredible economy of ammunition. Twenty of his later victories were achieved with an expenditure of only 130 rounds each.

With 40 Squadron he shot down twelve aircraft and on one occasion he scored eight victories on eight successive days. He also shot down three balloons in seventy-two hours.

He was awarded an MC in February 1918, a bar in March, and a second bar in April. He left 40 Squadron and took command of C Flight in 24 Squadron on February 19th 1918, scoring his first victory with the new squadron two days later. It was to be the first of eighteen victories with the squadron.

A crash on April 7th meant an enforced return to England to recover but in late June he came back to his favourite 40 Squadron with undiminished enthusiasm.

A DFC came in July and a bar followed within the month.

Deadly twin Spandaus on a Fokker DVll.

During combat over La Bassée on June 20th a broken connecting rod caused such vibration that the carburettor came adrift and caused a petrol fire. A long dive failed to extinguish it and he came down at Noeux les Mines, throwing himself out of the plane as it touched down and escaping with scratches and bruises.

With a score now standing at forty-nine he took off in the morning of July 31st from Bruay in his SE but never returned.

The manner of his death has never been known but he was buried at Laventie. Thus ended the career of one of the most successful pilots of the war.

Twin Vickers offset to port on Eddie Rickenbacker's Nieuport 28. Rickenbacker was America's highest scoring pilot.

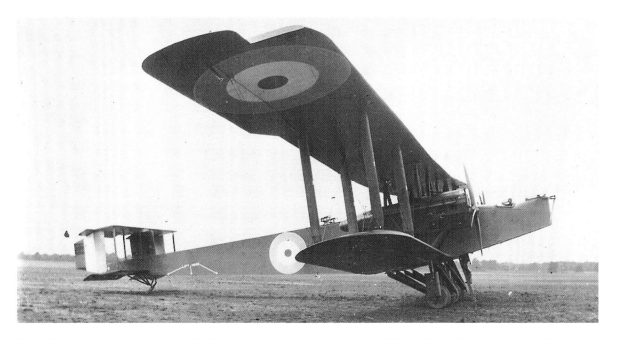

Handley Page heavy bomber, 100 ft wingspan. Powered by two 250 hp Rolls-Royce engines. F/Lt J. Alcock (later to fly the Atlantic non-stop) came down in the Aegean when piloting one and he and the rest of the crew were captured.

This appears to be an experimental Avro 529 powered by two 190 hp Rolls-Royce Falcons.

The DH4. A well-regarded two-seater bomber/reconnaissance aircraft with a 250 hp Rolls-Royce engine. Nearly 2,000 American-built machines reached France powered by the American 400 hp cylinder Liberty motor. A later development was the DH9.

21
ON LEAVE

Leave was eagerly awaited and thoroughly enjoyed. After living with constant fear and tension and under the shadow of death, it was an opportunity to forget the war and enjoy life to the full.

The first essential was to visit home and parents. Next the hedonistic pleasures of London.

The young pilots of 40 Squadron would often stay at the RFC Club or at Rosa Lewis's Cavendish Hotel in Jermyn Street. Both Lionel Blaxland and Sholto Douglas stayed there on occasion, though Mick Mannock and Jimmy McCudden favoured the RFC Club.

Rosa Lewis was a marvellous hostess with a free and easy outlook on life. She was considered to be King Edward VII's favourite cook and reputed to be one of his mistresses. She finally opened the Cavendish at the turn of the century.

The TV series 'The Duchess of Duke Street' was based on Rosa Lewis and the Cavendish. During the war she had a party in her sitting room every night where she loved to play hostess to the young RFC officers and pretty girls. The champagne flowed, conversation sparkled and everyone had a wonderful time.

How could these young people afford champagne? They couldn't! All of it was provided by Rosa who said that it would be put on the bill of wealthier clients but, no doubt, paid for by Rosa herself. Often enough, when the pilots were hard up at the end of their leaves, Rosa would waive the bill.

Autocratic, outspoken and notoriously undiplomatic there are a fund of stories about her. She would think nothing of loudly greeting an elderly peer with "Hello, Mutton Chops. Still fancy a nice, clean whore?"

On one occasion the Marquis of Bath took the wife of an American film director for a friendly drink when Rosa announced, for all to hear, that she had booked a room for them! In later life she banned Evelyn Waugh from the Cavendish after he featured her as Lottie Clump in *Vile Bodies*.

She eventually died aged 85 after a marvellous life and the Cavendish is no more.

So how did the young pilots spend their evenings in London? The musical theatre was an essential part of their visit and there was no shortage of hit shows to see. The music, gaiety and escapism was an antidote to the horrors of the Front.

Not to be missed were the musicals Chu Chin Chow and The Bing Boys at the Alhambra,

One of the most popular shows during the war years. The musical theatre played a vital role in maintaining morale. Alfred Lester and George Robey are featured on the cover.

two of the most successful shows in town which ran for most of the war years. Both of them were frequently mentioned in reminiscences of the Great War by all ranks. In the Bing Boys, George Robey and the beautiful Violet Loraine would sing *If You Were the only Girl in the World*, a nostalgic melody that still vividly brings to mind those wartime years and which is by no means forgotten today.

But there were many others: The Passing Show in which *I'll Make a Man of You* sung by Gwendoline Brocade, struck the spirit of the times and Maggie Smith sang it superbly three quarters of a century later in Joan Littlewood's 1969 film 'Oh, What a Lovely War'.

Also memorable was 'The Better 'Ole' by war cartoonist, Bruce Bairnsfather of Old Bill fame and

Arthur Elliot. Old Bill was an old sweat, a cartoon character invented by Bruce Bairnsfather who had a moustache like half a sweep's flue brush and was often featured at the Front up to his waist in water in an old shell hole, sorry, 'ole, philosophically and humorously reflecting on the situation.

There were lots of marvellous songs in these shows with many of them never to be forgotten. What do you *Want to Make Those Eyes at Me For (if they don't mean what they say)* from The Better 'Ole is surprisingly undated today.

So the young pilots would typically start off the evening with drinks at the Cavendish, then off to the Alhambra to see The Bing Boys followed by supper at Murrays or the Grafton Galleries.

After that it was up to the girls!

Leave was over all too soon, then it was back to France to climb into their cockpits once again to face that endless AA fire and the enemy machine-guns.

Jimmy McCudden in his SE5, or to give him his full title Major James J.B. McCudden VC, DSO and Bar, MC and Bar, MM, CDEG; fifty-seven victories. Joined the RFC as an air mechanic and was with the first unit to arrive in France in 1914. Died in an air accident on July 9th 1918. A friend of Mick Mannock, both were brought up in service families. *(Imperial War Museum)*

22

JIMMY MCCUDDEN

James Thomas Byford McCudden was a thinking pilot. By contrast Albert Ball would charge into an enemy squadron with machine-gun blazing regardless of the odds. Jimmy McCudden was very different.

He had come up the hard way. From air mechanic to observer and finally on to fighters. He was a perfectionist who took great care of his aircraft, its engine and guns. No impetuous rushes into combat for him. He carefully studied the whole new science of air fighting. He paid great attention to the enemy planes, pilots and their tactics.

In the air on solo flights he would carefully stalk his victims, only closing in for the kill at exactly the right moment when all the advantage lay with him.

He was not merely a solo flier but also a competent patrol leader, always ready to protect his fellow pilots and avoid unnecessary risks. Lionel had met him and was impressed by his modest manner. No bravado from Jimmy, despite his achievements.

Mick Mannock and Jimmy McCudden came from similar backgrounds. Both came from army families, were educated at army schools and, of course, both were from Irish stock. When they met they formed an instant rapport.

Jimmy joined the Royal Engineers as a bugler in 1910 transferring to the RFC in 1913. On the outbreak of war he had achieved the rank of Air Mechanic 1st Class and arrived in France in August 1914.

A sergeant by April 1915 he flew occasionally as an observer and even made a few unofficial flights as a pilot. His first combat as an observer was in December 1915.

In January 1916 he returned to England to learn to fly and that is where he met Mick Mannock. On completion of his flying training he joined 20 Squadron on July 1st 1916 flying FE2Ds. In August 1916 he was transferred to 29 Squadron as a fighter pilot flying DH2 pushers.

By the time he was sent back to Home Establishment in February 1917 he had fought successfully and had been awarded the Croix de Guerre and MC. He had also been commissioned. In England he served as a fighting instructor and a refresher course in France enabled him to fly Sopwith Pups.

In August 1917 with seven victories already achieved he joined the famous 56 Squadron as a flight commander flying SE5as.

From then on he rocketed to success and by February 1918 when he returned to Home

Establishment, his score stood at an amazing fifty-seven.

In the process, he had gained a bar to his MC, the VC, the DSO and bar and a bar to his MC.

After five months in England he was promoted to major and given command of the equally famous 60 Squadron.

Flying his SE to his new squadron in France he stopped briefly at Auxi le Chateau airfield but on take-off the engine of his SE cut out. Jimmy attempted to turn back but his plane side slipped into the ground, killing one of the most talented pilots of the war.

Anthony McCudden was determined to emulate his famous brother and was posted to Sholto Douglas's squadron. He was, however, hopelessly reckless and Jimmy was very worried about him. He remonstrated with him often enough and got in touch with Sholto several times concerned about Anthony's recklessness.

Sholto warned him frequently to exercise more caution but, of course, Anthony took no notice.

For a start he was by no means unsuccessful and Sholto recommended him for an MC which was awarded in March 1918. His final score stood at eleven victories.

"There are old pilots and bold pilots but there are no old, bold pilots," was a phrase not coined until much later in peacetime but, unfortunately, it applied to Anthony. Not long after the award of his MC he was shot down while the squadron was escorting another squadron on a bombing raid.

"He was far too brave and headstrong to make a successful fighter pilot," said Jimmy later, "for he was in the habit of doing daily over the enemy lines the most hair raising things."

The Martinsyde G100 'Elephant'. Designed as a long-range fighter with 120 hp Beardmore engine, later uprated to 160. åIt was found to be too big and heavy for a fighter and was relegated to bombing duties.

This is a captured Albatros D5.

The Armstrong Whitworth FK8 two-seater carried out similar work to the RE8, but was considered to be a better aeroplane which acquitted itself well against German fighters. Squadron crew called it the 'Big Ack'.

Newer fighters appeared towards the end of the war. This is a Sopwith Dolphin, first of the four-gun fighters. Span 32 ft 6 in. Length 22 ft 3 in. Engine 200 hp Hispano. Armament: twin Vickers and sometimes with the addition of twin Lewis. Maximum speed 117 mph at 17,000 ft. Service ceiling 19,000 ft.

Lionel's view. Sopwith Dolphin.

23
1918

So what happened in 1918? Newer and more efficient aircraft came into battle on both sides and in greatly increased numbers. A huge offensive by the Germans in 1918 pushed the allies back and almost achieved a breakthrough but, fortunately, it was fought to a standstill.

The SE5as, Sopwith Camels and Dolphins, and Bristol Fighters were in the forefront of the fighter attacks. The Germans had the new Albatros and the nimble Fokker Triplane which, in experienced hands such as Richthofen's, was a formidable fighter.

In the summer of 1918 the new Fokker D7 biplane started to appear, probably the best aircraft of the war. But America, too, was throwing her weight into the conflict both on the ground and in the air so the massive allied manpower and huge resources facing the Germans were bound to win in the end.

During August 1918 US Colonel Billy Mitchell persuaded the French to put a large part of their airforce at his disposal and was considered to have 701 fighters, 366 reconnaissance aircraft, 325 day bombers and ninety-one night bombers giving a total of 1,481 aircraft. He could also call on eight British bomber squadrons.

The Germans, however, had only 213 aircraft to oppose this huge force. Seventy-two fighters, twenty-four bombers, 105 reconnaissance planes, six ground attack aircraft and six long distance photography machines.

The British were pressing the Hindenburg line in early September and the French and Americans were due to launch their attack at St Mihiel on September 12th. Immediately after September 12th the Germans added four Jastas commanded by Oskar Von Boenigk and on the 28th JG1 arrived commanded by Herman Göring. But despite their far inferior numbers the German planes still managed to inflict tremendous losses on their opponents. September 1918 was to be the worst month of all in World War One for allied aircraft losses and was forever known as 'Black September'.

This, amazingly, was within only six weeks of the armistice and even more suprisingly the Germans were desperately short of all supplies, everything from petrol to ammunition. They were also handicapped by the shortage of replacement pilots. Shortage of petrol, in fact, limited the sorties they could make.

Many of the German aces who flew in spring 1917 had been killed including Manfred von Richthofen, Werner Voss, Kurt Wolff, Karl Allmenroder, Karl Emil-Schaffer and others but

Göring, Loerzer, von Schleich, Buckler, Greimm, Jacobs, and Thuy were still flying together with Ernst Udet, second only to Richthofen in victories. Lothar von Richthofen had also survived after scoring forty victories but was to be killed in a flying accident in 1922.

On the British side, however, there were very few men still flying in France who had flown in spring 1917. Those that had survived were back in England instructing or in non-flying jobs.

So September 1918 was the final lash of the dragon's tail. Soon the aircrew who survived would be back in defeated and demoralised Germany, short of food and resources, riven by civil unrest and with communist gangs roaming the streets. Astronomic inflation would soon follow.

The British air services were to return, victorious, to "A land fit for heroes" but that is another story!

Sopwith Snipe. The final development of Sopwith's rotary-engined fighters. Span 31 ft 1 in. Length 19 ft 10 in. Engine 230 hp Bentley BR2. Armament: twin Vickers. Speed 121 mph at 10,000 ft. Service ceiling 19,500 ft.

Sopwith Snipe.

This was No. 61 Home Defence Aerodrome to which Lionel was posted after his service in France.

24

LIONEL BLAXLAND'S SUBSEQUENT FLYING CAREER

Lionel's last flights in France with 40 Squadron were on July 12th 1917 when he flew three patrols at noon, 2pm and 7.39 pm.

These flights were packed with incidents: Firstly he had to land at Naval 8's airfield with engine trouble and on a later patrol engine trouble again forced him to land. Enemy aircraft engaged and he fired two bursts at one, seeing tracers hit it but no certain result. On another occasion an enemy aircraft got on the tail of his Nieuport but a fellow Nieuport drove it off.

So that ended his flying in France.

Back in England he was posted to 61 Home Defence Squadron so now, at last, his hazardous flying days were over... or so you would have thought. But you would have been absolutely mistaken. Flying the unreliable planes of those days with so many forced landings was almost as dangerous as facing the Germans.

On August 15th he flew with his new squadron for the first time. His machine was the Sopwith Pup. On October 19th flying a Sopwith Pup on balloon practice the engine failed when he was over the sea and he made an emergency landing on Southend Pier, shorting out the electric railway! Surely one of the most unusual landings of the war. The Pup was a write-off but Lionel was unhurt.

From October onwards he flew all types of aircraft: DH2s, more Pups, FE8s, BE 2Cs, and an SE5a for the first time on November 14th. Before the end of his service he was even to fly a Sopwith Snipe, the most advanced British rotary-engined fighter of the war.

Patrols and night flying took up much of his time. Night flying was in its infancy in those days and was very hazardous indeed. Two forced landings occurred in December, but he was unhurt. His first night flight on a SE5a was on January 2nd 1918. There was a false air raid alarm at 3.30pm on January 28th and although he returned safely a pilot named Mason crashed at Woolwich.

At 9.35pm on the same day he was in the air in earnest to intercept a Gotha (pronounced Goat-ah) raid. Stacy and Young engaged the Gothas and fired at them but with little apparent effect but they saw a Gotha shot down in flames near Benfleet by Captain Blackwell and S.C. Banks of 44 Squadron. On another night raid on January 29th, firstly the engine of his SE5a failed after leaving the ground at 11.15pm but, fortunately, he landed safely. Off again at 11.40pm he saw no enemy aircraft and had to land in the mist running over two flairs that indicated the landing ground but, again, without damage.

Southend-on-Sea taken from an Avro. Lionel Blaxland landed his Sopwith Pup on Southend pier – on the electric railway. The engine had cut out. The undercarriage was swept off it and it sustained other damage – this happened when shooting at small balloons over the river.

Patrols and night flying continued through to the spring. On April 26th a night patrol in misty conditions proved hazardous. Flying a BE2C he overshot the aerodrome and turned over in a ploughed field. He was suspended in his machine upside down for ten minutes but escaped unscathed. Collins and MacVickers also crashed with MacVickers's plane bursting into flames but he escaped unhurt.

On May 19th came another raid: 200 aircraft were reputedly observed although Lionel saw none! Four Gothas were shot down by AA fire and British aircraft.

152

61 Squadron. Lorry to Shoeburyness.

61 Squadron. RAF F.C. 1918/19. From left to right: Pumphrey, Kinsey, LBB, ?, Faulkner, Lofthouse, Morrison?

Fellow pilots at Rochford

F. A. Pumphrey

H.A. Blain

Captain R.W. Young (Dixie)

L. Greenwood

There was a forced landing again on May 19th but he again got out unhurt. It must have been about this time that he flew the 'Comic Camel'; a Sopwith Camel that had been unofficially converted into a two-seater. He was to fly it again later so what was it like to fly? Pass! I am afraid I never asked Lionel about it as I knew nothing of it until his nephew John Simpkinson told me about it after Lionel's death. During Chris Draper's time in Naval 8 in 1918 they also converted a Camel into a two-seater and apparently flew it successfully but when the authorities heard about it they were quickly told to put it back to the original.

In June he made his first cross channel flight in a SE5a, landing at Marguise and night flying continued through the month with more forced landings. On August 1st a wheel came off his Sopwith Camel on take-off and he crashed it when attempting to land but was again unhurt. Flights continued through August and September, mostly on Sopwith Camels.

The war ended on November 11th 1918 but Lionel continued to fly, fortunately without incident, until his last flight on a Camel on March 3rd 1919 ending his RAF service.

There is, however, a sequel. On the back page of his flying log book he enumerates the crashes and forced landings in his flying career. Although no longer in the RAF he lists the following flights after the war:

Sopwith two-seater	Repton (Derbyshire)	1924
Bristol Fighter	Old Sarum	August 1927
Sparters three-seater	Hitchin	April 1921
Avro	Cresswell	March 1932
Hawker Hart		March 1938
Anson Harvard Magister	Little Rissington	August 1940
Burnaston (Derby)	(Dual with F. Lt. Brown. Did 3 landings and won registered dual comp.)	
Whitney 45 mins	Ashbourne	July 1943

Accidents did happen:

BE2E. After hitting house and scaffolding.

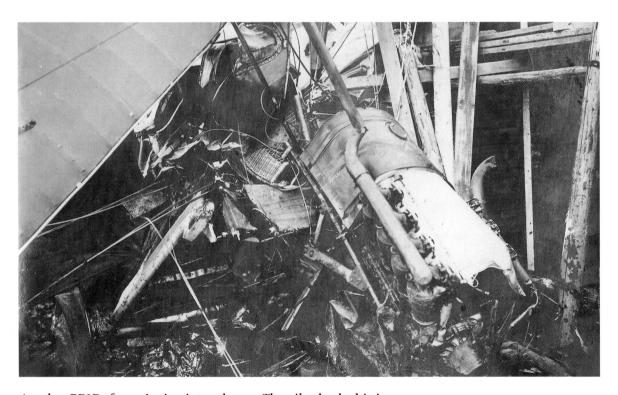

Another BE2E after spinning into a house. The pilot broke his jaw.

Comic Camel Night Fighter. This was a Camel converted to a two-seater. Lionel claimed that it flew quite well.

The two-seater Sopwith. Another view of the comic Camel.

The war is over. Happy days are here again! Lionel on the Rudge Multi with possibly brother Arthur on the pillion? Lionel and his friends were all keen motorcyclists and at last the open road beckoned.

Lionel's caption reads simply "Gussie", obviously an old friend. He is astride the Rudge Multi.

Harley Davidson 1919. Luxury on three wheels for those days. Just look at the racy lines of the sidecar and that generous screen for the passenger.

House party 7 Dec 1918, Vernons, East Barnet. ("Sammy") Somerville, Winnie Vasey, Mrs V, Mr & Mrs ?, "Monte", – , Joan V, – , – ,

P Vernon, Wolff V, LBB, Baker, Briggs, Kennith Norwood

Lionel's caption reads: 'This Bloody War is over at last and here is a house party to celebrate. The uniforms will soon be finally put away and a Brave New World beckons.' What will the future hold for them all?

The end of the war saw designers rushing to their drawing boards to design ultra-light aircraft powered by motorcycle engines. The RAF clearly bought one and here it is, named kitten, and piloted by Captain Henderson.

The famous *Le Pou de Ciel* the Flying Flea of 1934. Safe enough in its designer's hands but dangerous with inexperienced pilots so, once again, the dream was never realised.

25

Après La Guerre Finis

Aeroplane development had rocketed during the period 1914-18 and the number of planes flying had grown out of all recognition.

Immediately after the First World War it was expected that flying for everyman would arrive. The way forward was, they thought, in tiny aeroplanes powered by motorcycle engines that could take off from a farmer's field. The skies would be filled by everyone buzzing around the skies in these ultra-light aeroplanes.

Designers sharpened their pencils and did, indeed, come up with a vast array of minute, motorcycle-engined planes. Avro, for example, designed their tiny Avro Babe and the redoubtable Bert Hinkler, former wartime pilot and later long distance flyer, flew it from England to Milan. No small feat with a plane powered with a Douglas motorcycle engine.

In 1924 there was a contest for these flying tiddlers and there was no shortage of entries. Bert Hinkler flew a very workmanlike Avro Avia, not to be confused with the later full sized Avro Avian. The Avia was powered by a Douglas motorcycle engine and, believe it or not, was a two-seater.

One of Lionel Blaxland's photographs taken shortly after the war was of a 'Kitten'. A really tiny little plane.

Fellow muzzle loader Edward Chadfield used to run a clay pigeon shoot in Derbyshire but has since moved to Scotland which suits Edward and his wife very well indeed. He has a propeller stamped 'Sopwith Cygnet' which came from the former Derby airport at Burnaston.

On page 164 I include a contemporary photograph of the Cygnet which was designed by the great Sydney Camm who went on to design the Hurricane.

Few of these early 1920s ultra-light aircraft can have survived and, reputedly, only two Avro Cygnets were ever made but one of them, amazingly, has survived and is on show at the RAF museum at Cosford.

So those early ultra-lights powered by motorcycle engines were never a success and did not, at the end of the day, provide low cost flying for everyman. They were found to be too underpowered to be safe.

Later in the 1920s an opportunity to fly at comparatively modest cost was provided by flying clubs but in those lean years even the modest cost put it out of reach of most people. The De Haviland Tiger Moth was a favoured choice of the clubs. But in 1933 the possibility of a tiny plane at low cost, again powered by a motorcycle engine, seemed about to become a reality. A Frenchman named Henri Mignet designed and flew his *Le Pou de Ciel*, the Flea of the Sky, known in England as the Flying Flea. It was an unlikely looking aeroplane, reminiscent of a pram with a large wing on top!

The Flea could be built for about £100, including a suitable engine, and Monsieur Mignet flew his successfully without accidents.

The snag was that it was not accident free in the hands of other home builders. It required very skilful handling otherwise it could spin disastrously out of control with fatal consequences. A number of such accidents meant that a Certificate of Airworthiness could no longer be granted to Flying Fleas.

A great attempt but, unfortunately, doomed to failure and with the demise of the Flying Flea went the hopes of the home builder of miniature aircraft.

In 1923/24 the Avro Avis 2-seater was successfully flown by the great Bert Hinkler. It was powered by a 6 hp Douglas motorcycle engine.

1930s ultra-lightweights

American Aeronca side by side two-seater powered by a 36 hp engine.

BAC Drone. Pusher airscrew driven by an 18 hp Douglas engine.

The Hawker Cygnet powered by the Watt Cherub engine. Designed by the great Sydney Camm (left) who later designed the Hurricane. Bulmer, Hawker's chief test pilot is on the right. Reputedly only two were made but one survives at Cosford. *(Photograph lent by Edward Chadfield who also owns a Cygnet propeller)*

APPENDIX ONE
THE WARTIME SONGS

The people were all brought up in a time of moral certainty with no doubt that the British Empire was the greatest that the world had ever known. After all, didn't we 'own' the huge area on the map of the world coloured pink?

Most of the soldiers, sailors and airmen had been brought up in the strict Christian religion. Church on Sunday was essential: in some families as much as three times in the day. Sunday School and bible class for the children and membership of the Boys Brigade and Church Lads Brigade was open to all.

Their sports, sing-songs and camaraderie bound them together and meetings would end with a hymn and a prayer. Summer camps, picnics and Christmas socials completed the bonding.

Boy Scouts, too, followed the Christian ethic though the cost of the uniform restricted membership to more affluent families.

So the Christian spirit and love of music and singing united all. Every family who could afford it, and some who couldn't, had a piano in the 'front room' and musical evenings for family and friends round the piano were a vital part of society. Aunt Agatha would sing *Come into the Garden Maud*, Uncle Bill in basso-profundo voice, would sing his party piece from 'The Gondoliers' and all would join in singing the popular songs of the day. During the war different songs would come to the fore.

The popular songs were, of course, common to all the services and the home front. There are a number of those songs that enshrine the spirit of the war but, perhaps, *Keep the Home Fires Burning, Roses of Picardy, Tipperary* and *The Long, Long Trail* are among the most evocative.

Keep the Home Fires Burning, originally entitled *Till the Boys Come Home* was written in 1914 by twenty-one-year-old Royal Naval Air Services pilot, Ivor Novello with words by American poet Lena Guilbert Ford. Ivor was later to claim that he had written some of them, however.

After crashing two aeroplanes Ivor was given a desk job at RFC Headquarters in London as his value as a patriotic songwriter was considered to be of more importance than his habit of busting aeroplanes.

He was, indeed, a prolific song writer and playwright, writing West End Revues. During the war he composed over fifty songs and went on to even greater successes for decades afterwards.

Despite the enormous success of the song, Lena Guilbert Ford earned nothing from it and was, surprisingly, killed together with her young son by a Zeppelin bomb in 1918.

No doubt you know the words but, just in case, this is the chorus:

Keep the home fires burning,
While your hearts are yearning,
Though your lads are far away they dream of home.
There's a silver lining
Through the dark cloud shining,
Turn the dark cloud inside out
Till the boys come home.

This song had an enormous emotional impact throughout the war as practically every family in the land had a family member go to war. Played on a battered mouth organ by a homesick Tommy crouched in a freezing, muddy, front line dugout during a dark, winter night with only a flickering candle for illumination, it must have been heart-rending. *Roses of Picardy* was another deeply moving song written in 1916 by Haydn Wood with words by Fred Weatherby. It conveys the deep sorrows of parting.

Roses are shining in Picardy,
In the hush of the silvery dew.
Roses are flow'ring in Picardy,
But there's never a rose like you!
And the roses will die with the summertime,
And our roads may be far apart,
But there's one rose that dies not in Picardy!
T'is the rose that I keep in my heart!

The Long, Long Trail was another nostalgic melody that, although written in 1912 by the American, Zo Elliott, came into its own during the war and encapsulated the spirit of the times.

There's a long, long trail a-winding into the land of my dreams,
where the nightingales are singing and a white moon beams:
There's a long, long night of waiting
Until my dreams all come true:
Till the day when I'll be going down
That long, long trail with you.

But not all songs were sentimental: There were rousing songs, cheerful songs, comic songs, marching songs, derisive songs and many parodies of other songs and hymns. Siegfried Sassoon wrote about two Tommies marching past their elderly general inspecting them on their way to the front:

"He's a cheery old card, said Harry to Jack as they marched up to Arras with rifle and pack. But he did for them both with his plan of attack!"

'TILL THE BOYS COME HOME

SONG

WORDS BY

LENA GUILBERT FORD

MUSIC BY

IVOR NOVELLO

PRICE 1/6 NET, CASH.

ASCHERBERG. HOPWOOD & CREW, LTD.
IN WHICH ARE INCORPORATED THE CATALOGUES OF
E. ASCHERBERG & C°   JOHN BLOCKLEY.   DUNCAN DAVISON & C°
HOPWOOD & CREW. LT°   HOWARD & C°   ORSBORN & TUCKWOOD.
16. MORTIMER STREET, REGENT STREET.
LONDON. W.

NEW YORK: LEO FEIST, INC.

Copyright, MCMXIV, by Ascherberg, Hopwood & Crew, Ltd.

PRINTED IN ENGLAND.

Originally *Till the Boys Come Home*, but better known later as *Keep the Home Fires Burning*. One of the most popular songs of 1914 – 1918.

It's a Long Way to Tipperary vividly brings to mind Tommies singing as they marched cheerfully to the Front, blissfully ignorant of what fate had in store for them when they got there.

The song was written by a market stall holder named Judge who wrote it for a bet. It made him a lot of money including a pension until his death in 1938. He was not born in Ireland but his grandparents were.

The song was first sung by the Connaught Rangers who had been stationed in Tipperary before the war. A *Daily Mail* correspondent, George Curnock, heard it in Boulogne in 1914 "as a company of Connaught Rangers passed us singing with a note of strange pathos in their rich, Irish voices, a song that I had never heard before." His report alerted the world to this evocative song that went on to achieve immortality.

It's a long way to Tipperary,
It's a long way to go;
It's a long way to Tipperary,
To the sweetest girl I know!
Goodbye Piccadilly,
Farewell Leicester Square,
It's a long, long way to Tipperary,
But my heart's right there!

One of the most famous of the Great War songs has to be *Pack up Your Troubles in Your Old Kit Bag*. It was written in 1915 by George Asat and Felix Powell. Lucifers (matches) were scarce in France and were badly needed for lighting everything from fires to gaspers (cigarettes). They had to be sent over to France under the same conditions as shells and explosives so that didn't help their availability!

Pack up your troubles in your old kit bag
And smile, smile, smile.
While you've a Lucifer to light your fag,
Smile boys, that's your style.
What's the use of worrying?
It never was worth while,
So pack up your troubles in your old kit bag,
And smile, smile, smile.

A personal favourite is *Good-bye-ee*. Slang of the period is included: Toodle-oo, cheerio and chin-chin, for example, together with the wartime napoo. This is the anglicised version of "il n'y en a plus" (there is none left).

Good-bye-ee! Good-bye-ee!
Wipe the tear, baby dear,
From your eye-ee.

One of Ivor Novello's songs from the 1916 revue, 'Theodore & Co.' at the Gaiety Theatre.

Though it's hard to part, I know,
I'll be tickled to death to go.
Don't cry-ee! Don't sigh-ee!
There's a silver lining in the sky-ee.
Bonsoir, old thing!
Cheerio! Chin-chin!
Napoo! Toodle-oo! Good-bye-ee!

A derisive favourite is *But For Gawd's Sake Don't Send Me*, written by Gitz Rice in 1917 as *The Conscientious Objector's Lament* and sung by Alfred Lester in the review 'Round the Map'. Written to ridicule conscientious objectors it always threatened to bring the house down. Enthusiastically sung by soldiers at the Front:

Send out the Army and the Navy,
Send out the rank and file,
Send out the brave old Territorials
They'll face the danger with a smile.
Send out the Boys of the Old Brigade,
Who made Old England free,
Send out me brother, me sister and me mother
But for Gawd's sake don't send me!

There were, of course, many more songs of the war years, here are a few of them: *Hitchy Koo, Send Him a Cheerful Letter, Take Me Back To Dear Old Blighty, Oh! It's a Lovely War, Old Soldiers Never Die, Fred Karno's Army, Hanging On The Old Barbed Wire, Mademoiselle From Armenteers* (of which there were over fifty versions, nearly all unprintable!), *Après La Guerre Fini*, and, of course the unforgettable *When This Bloody War Is Over.*

APPENDIX TWO

SONGS OF THE ROYAL FLYING CORPS

Lionel Blaxland vividly remembered everyone in the mess gathering round the piano and lustily singing those songs of World War One and, in particular, the RFC ones….until playing that battered piano was considered to result in a death sentence. But even that superstition was eventually forgotten and the singing started again.

As well as the usual songs of the time the RFC had a few of their own. One of the oldest and best known of them all was *The Dying Aviator*. This dated back to 1912 when the RFC was formed from the balloon section of the Royal Engineers. There were a number of verses linked by three main choruses. The first verse and the three main choruses are listed below:

> *Oh, the bold aviator lay dying,*
> *And as 'neath the wreckage he lay, he lay,*
> *To the sobbing mechanics about him,*
> *These last dying words did he say:*
> *Two valve springs you'll find in my stomach,*
> *Three spark plugs are safe in my lung,*
> *The prop is in splinters inside me,*
> *To my fingers the joystick has clung.*
>
> *Take the propeller boss out of my liver,*
> *Take the aileron out of my thigh, my thigh,*
> *From the seat of my pants take the piston,*
> *Then see if the old crate will fly.*
> *Take the cylinders out of my kidneys,*
> *The connecting rod out of my brain, my brain,*
> *From the small of my back take the crankshaft*
> *And assemble the engine again.*

My personal favourite of the RFC songs is *What Did You Want To Have A Crash Like That For?* to the tune of *What Do You Want To Make Those Eyes At Me For?* from Bruce Bairnsfather's 1916 review, 'A Better 'Ole'.

What did you want to have a crash like that for?
It's the sixth you've had today.
It makes you sad, it makes me mad,
It's lucky it was an Avro, not a brand new Spad.
What did you want to have a crash like that for?
You'd better clear the wreckage all away,
But never mind, you'll go up again tonight
With umpteen bombs all loaded with dynamite,
And if you have another crash like that one,
It's the LAST you'll have today.

Another favourite song of the RFC to the tune of *D'ye Ken John Peel* was *We Haven't got a Hope In The Morning*:

When you soar through the air in a Sopwith Scout,
And you're scrapping with a Hun and your gun cuts out,
Well, you stuff down your nose till your plugs fall out,
cos' you haven't got a hope in the morning.
For a batman woke me from my bed,
I'd had a thick night and a very sore head,
And I said to myself, to myself I said,
Oh we haven't got a hope in the morning!

One of 54 Squadron's favourite songs was *Dirty Danny's Digging Deeper Dugouts*. The tune was from *Sister Susie's Sewing Shirts For Soldiers*. This is how it went:

Dirty Danny's digging deeper dugouts,
Much deeper dug-outs Danny dug to make a fug.
One day he dug a topper,
But the General came a cropper
In that damn, deeper, dugout Danny dug.
Heavy handed Hans flies Halberstadters,
In handy Halberstadters for a flight our Hans does start;
His Oberst says, "O dash it,
For I fear that he will crash it,
See how heavy-handed Hans ham-handles handy Halberstadts.

Now I'm A General At The Ministry was a parody on *I am the Ruler of the Queen's Navee* from 'HMS Pinafore' by Gilbert and Sullivan. First and last verse below:

When I was a boy I went to war,
As an air mechanic in the Flying Corps,
I dished out dope and I swung the prop,
And I polished up my talents in the fitters' shop;
And I did my work so carefully
That now I'm a General at the Ministry.
I flew in France with such amazing zest
That the King grew tired of adorning my chest,
People boosted McCudden, Bishop and Ball,
But readily agreed that I out-soared them all.

My merits were declared so overwhelmingly
That now I'm a General at the Ministry.
So mechanics all, wherever you be,
If you want to climb to the top of the tree,
If your soul isn't fettered to a pail of dope,
Just take my tip – there's always hope,
Be smart in the Strand at saluting me
And you'll be a General at the Ministry.

Another favourite was *We Are the Ragtime RFC* though an alternative was *We Are the Ragtime Army*.

We are the Ragtime Flying Corps,
We are the Ragtime boys,
We are respected by every nation
And we're loved by all the girls (I don't think!),
People, they think we're millionaires,
Think we're dealers in stocks and shares;
When we go out the people roar
We are the Ragtime Flying Corps.

We are the Ragtime Flying Corps, We are the RFC.
We spend our tanners, we know our manners,
And are respected wherever we go.
Walking up and down the Farnborough Road,
Doors and windows open wide.
We are the boys of the RFC
We don't care a damn for Germany:
We are the Flying Corps.

Finally:

When this bloody war is over
No more soldiering for me.
When I get my civvy clothes on,
Oh how happy I shall be!

"The music, the laughter and, above all, the songs of the First World War, have been described as 'a protest of life against death' but perhaps they merely represent the ascendancy of the human spirit over the cruel inhumanity of the war itself. The songs are still remembered and, some still sung almost a century after the start of that 'Great War' that still haunts succeeding generations. That surely is a kind of immortality and, in a sense, a fitting memorial to those men who marched to war in a forgotten world."[2]

2 Lynne MacDonald, the highly acclaimed World War One historian.

Left: Ivor Novello in the uniform of a flight
sub-lieutenant Royal Naval Air Service 1916
with his beloved 'Mam'.

APPENDIX THREE
THE MOTORCYCLES

Motorcycles are frequently featured in the reminiscences of RFC pilots and often merit a mention in these pages. Many pilots, including Lionel Blaxland, were motorcyclists and they frequently borrowed machines to see crashed planes or to visit other aerodromes. These motorcycles would probably have been RFC P&Ms.

In World War One a favourite motorcycle with army dispatch riders was the $2^3/_4$ hp Douglas. They were horizontally opposed side-valve twins with the cylinders in line with the frame. Two speeders with chain drive from engine to gearbox then belt drive from gearbox to rear wheel: not so good in Flanders mud! No kick start so they had to be push-started or 'paddled off' with the rider sitting on the saddle. Even so, the dispatch riders claimed they were easy starters.

Triumph also produced motorcycles for the armed forces: the 4 hp 550cc single-cylinder side-valve Model H. It had the advantage of a three-speed gearbox and kickstart, with chain drive from engine to gearbox but belt drive from the gearbox to rear wheel. 20,000 were made for the British services and 10,000 for the Allies.

The RFC, however, used $3^1/_2$hp P&Ms. Single-cylinder side-valve with two speeds but all chain drive. The rear chain, in addition, was enclosed in a chaincase which was a tremendous advantage. They were also ahead of the Douglas as they had a kick-start. Years later P&Ms were to change their name to Panther. The RFC had their own mobile motorcycle workshops in France to repair their P&Ms and machines too badly damaged to be repaired in them were returned to England to be repaired in special RFC motorcycle workshops or returned to the manufacturer for repair.

These hp designations were the old nominal RAC ratings and nothing to do with the actual horse-power produced. All 350cc machines were designated as $2^3/_4$ hp and 500cc $3^1/_2$ hp. When I first started motorcycling, old timers still spoke of a $2^3/_4$ and a $3^1/_2$ and, in case you ask, a 250cc was a $2^1/_2$ hp.

Over 25,000 350cc Douglas motorcycles were supplied to the armed forces between 1914 and 1918. Light, rugged and reliable. Two speed, no kick start. This is a dispatch rider in France.

The RFC and later Royal Air Force used 500 cc P&Ms. This is a servicewoman on a Panther and sidecar. No doubt a chauffeuse to high-ranking RAF officers.

Right: A Vee Twin Clyno machine-gun outfit. Note the reversed seat so that the gun could be fired either way. I cannot see that such combinations were of practical use though in World War Two, German Panzer combinations were highly effective during the Blitzkreig.

Below: Flying and motorcycling always did go together. This is wartime pilot J. Alcock RN with his 1914 TT Douglas. He was later to gain fame, and a knighthood, when he and his colleague Arthur Whitten Brown were the first people to make a non-stop flight across the Atlantic in 1919.

APPENDIX FOUR
THE MACHINE-GUN

The sand of the desert is sodden red,
Red with the wreck of a square that broke;
The Gatling's jammed and the Colonel dead,
And the regiment blind with dust and smoke.
The river of death has brimmed his banks ...

These lines by Sir Henry Newbolt convey the spirit of the scene in the late nineteenth century: Soldiers fighting a desperate battle against all the odds with their most important weapon, the Gatling, out of action.

Multiple fire had been the unattainable objective for centuries and James Puckle had invented a flintlock machine-gun in 1718 but did it ever really work?

Many others had tried but the first practical machine-gun was made by Richard Gatling in 1862. It had six barrels that revolved and were fed by cartridges from a hopper. Turning a crank handle fired each barrel in turn and if the hopper was constantly refilled fifty shots a minute could be achieved. You must have seen many Westerns in which, at the eleventh hour, the devastating fire from a Gatling knocked down the Indians like ninepins! So a practical, simple and effective machine-gun had arrived at last, though not suitable for aeroplanes when they came along. But could a machine-gun be devised where part of the explosive force of the bullet could be used to eject the old cartridge case, feed another cartridge into the breech and activate the firing pin? A truly automatic gun.

The brilliant American inventor, Hiram Maxim, solved the problem. He took out his first patents in 1883 and the Maxim Gun Company was formed in November 1884. A demonstration in England achieved 670 rounds a minute.

Maxim sold his machine-guns everywhere – except in his home country the United States as the US Government was not interested. Manufacture and development in England was taken on by the Vickers company and by 1914 the gun was known as the Vickers. They were to continue into the 1960s.

In Germany, too, the deadly and effective Spandaus were a development of the Maxim. Kaiser Wilhelm II, Emperor of Germany, saw the Maxims demonstrated at Spandau in the

Opposite page: Joseph Frantz, flying a Voisin, makes the first known kill in aerial combat, October 5th, 1914. From an original painting by John Batchelor.

1890s. Spandau was the Berlin district famous for armament manufacture.

Against the Maxim were the Gatling, a Nordenfeldt, and a Gardner, all of which had to be hand cranked. The Maxim outperformed them all with a rate of fire of 600 rounds a minute. It was also more accurate. "That is the gun – there can be no other!" opined the Kaiser. The British machine-guns fired the standard .303 cartridge as used in the .303 short Lee Enfield rifle. The German machine-guns also used the standard 7.91 (approximately .311 inch) cartridge as employed in the infantryman's 1898 Mauser. This rifle action is still in use in sporting rifles today. With weight being all-important the obvious choice for aircraft was the lightweight Lewis so how many did the RFC have at the start of the war in 1914. Was it 100? 200? 500? No, none of these, just a solitary one!

It must be remembered that in August 1914 the RFC was tiny; a mere fraction of what it what it was eventually to become. Also in those early days the role of aircraft was considered to be reconnaissance only. There was no conception of a fighting role.

The Germans, however, did not use a Lewis equivalent but relied on the efficient, and deadly, belt-fed Spandau. The Spandau firing through the propeller with the help of Anthony Fokker's interrupter gear on the Fokker Eindekkers (monoplanes) in 1915 brought a new dimension to air warfare. By the end of the year the German biplane fighters, such as the Albatros, had twin Spandaus.

The first Allied airman to use a machine-gun firing through the propeller was the Frenchman, Roland Garros. Today's sports stadium in Paris is named after him. Back in 1912 he had set an altitude record of 15,000 feet, astonishing for those early days.

He had reasoned that only 2% of bullets would hit the rotating propeller so he had steel deflector plates fitted to the propeller of his machine which enabled him to fire forwards through it from April 1st 1915. This system brought him great success and when he eventually force-landed in enemy territory due to engine failure on April 18th they examined the propeller with great care.

Anthony Fokker was a brilliant Dutchman who was twenty-four years old when war broke out but he had already designed and flown his own machines. Fokker offered his services to Holland, France and Britain but none were interested so he worked for Germany.

He was asked if he could improve on Garros's crude design and he quickly came up with a true interrupter gear. With propellers rotating at 1,200 a minute this gave a six-inch clear space for bullets 2,400 times a minute.

It was first fitted to the Fokker Eindekker and in the hands of pilots like Boelcke and Immelmann it gave the Germans mastery of the skies from August 1915 onwards.

Surprisingly, however, although Fokker was the first man to design and install an interrupter gear during the war the idea was not new. Details of an interrupter gear had been published in the April 1914 issue of the *Scientific American*, though no-one took any notice, and before the war a Swiss engineer, Franz Schneider, had patented an interrupter gear. The Russian Lieutenant Poplavko had developed an interrupter gear in 1913 and the English Edwards brothers submitted their plans for an interrupter gear to the War Office in early 1914 but it was not interested. These pioneers were not alone as other inventors had worked on interrupter systems.

The British, however, were way behind the Germans. The first efforts were in pusher machines with the propeller behind the pilot so that a forward-firing Lewis gun could be used.

Next came tractor aircraft with a Lewis gun mounted on the top plane: clumsy and inconvenient.

The first British fighter to have a synchronised Vickers gun was the Sopwith $1^1/_2$ Strutter which came into service in April 1916. The observer had a Lewis gun. But, even then, the top brass didn't get the message. The nimble Nieuports should have had a synchronised Vickers or, better still, twin Vickers, but had to make do with a single Lewis on the top plane.

You would have thought that the success of the German machines with single synchronised guns in 1915 and twin guns in 1916 would have spurred the British authorities to follow suit, but these lessons were ignored.

When the state-of-the-art SE5a arrived in April 1917 it still had that damned Lewis on the top plane and only a single Vickers firing through the propeller so it was under-gunned by comparison with its opponents and it never did get twin Vickers. It was not until the arrival of the Sopwith Camel in July 1917 that twin Vickers guns were fitted to a British aeroplane.

But why didn't they work?

Reading pilots' accounts of World War One combats you discover, with depressing regularity: "The machine-gun stopped firing after a few rounds." This is invariably the case with British machine-guns but it very seldom appeared to happen with German ones.

It must have been horrifying to go into combat, have the enemy machine in your sights and open fire only to have your gun jam, leaving you unarmed with the enemy pilot free to fire at you as he pleased.

But why was it? Would the answer have been to copy the German Spandaus with their seemingly greater reliability? But, on reflection, they were both developments of the Maxims and the Lewis guns were just as bad.

I have puzzled over this question for years and have finally concluded that the problem was down to the quality of the ammunition. If a cartridge failed to fire then the next cartridge could not load so a dud cartridge would stop the gun. Although all ammunition destined for the RFC was visually inspected it could not be predicted that a particular percussion cap would fail to fire. It would appear, then, that the quality of the German ammunition was better.

Have you ever heard of the American doctor Samuel N. McClean? He was a doctor who was also a keen inventor. He turned his attention to the design of a machine-gun because he reasoned that: "A machine-gun is a noble thing as the mechanism which accomplishes the greatest amount of human destruction in the shortest possible time with the least difficulty may make war obsolete, for what rational man would throw his life away senselessly in front of one?" Sadly, however, this noble and optimistic prediction was far wide of the mark in the killing fields of the Western Front.

He did, indeed, design and make a machine-gun but it still required development. His lack of success forced him out of his own company and all his patents were taken over by the Automatic Arms Company which was formed in 1910.

This brings us to another American, Isaac Newton Lewis. He was born in October 1858 and reputedly named after the great British scientist. He joined the army and graduated at West Point in 1884. Engineering design was his forte and he finally attained the rank of colonel. He toured Europe at the start of the twentieth century having been instructed to assess all European ordnance: no small task. He started on the development of the McClean gun for the Automatic

Arms Company and eventually joined the company.

He left the army in 1913 and in 1914 he sailed to Europe taking four of the now developed guns with him. He successfully demonstrated the guns and half a dozen arms manufacturers started production. Predictably the American government was not interested.

In Belgium the Armes Automatique Lewis was formed to manufacture the guns and in Britain the Birmingham Small Arms Company not only took over manufacture but bought more land on which to build another factory to produce them.

By March 1915 BSA were producing 100 guns a week, by the end of the year this had risen to 300 a week and by March 1916 it was 500 a week.

The American government finally did wake up and in May 1917, a month after America declared war on Germany, they placed huge orders for Lewis guns in .300 calibre. Colonel Lewis, however, had always said that he would not make profits out of his own government and he was to honour that pledge.

The Garros Wedge. Steel plates on the propeller to deflect bullets.

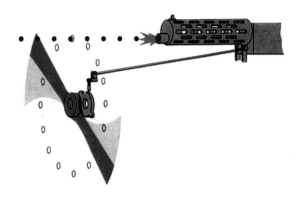

The principle of the Fokker interrupter gear which blocked the firing mechanism when the propeller was in line with the bullet.

The Lewis guns supplied to the army weighed under 27 lbs and were fed by a circular drum holding 47 rounds. The stripped-down Lewis as supplied to the RFC only weighed $17^1/_2$ lbs and had a drum containing 97 rounds. I understand that all Lewis guns supplied to the RFC and RAF during World War One were manufactured by BSA, and they were the mainstay of the RFC during the first years of the war. Lewis guns were to continue in use during the two world wars.

APPENDIX FIVE

DOUGLASS WHETTON

Douglass Whetton's life was devoted to World War One aviation and he had studied the whole subject in immense detail, undistracted by work, wife or children.

He lived in a semi-detached house with his mother in Littleover on the outskirts of Derby. Did he have any kind of job? Not that I know of, so how he managed financially I have no idea.

But his in-depth researches were exhaustive. He did not accept any established views but reached conclusions of his own.

Mannock's official score, for example, was seventy-three victories and considered to be unofficially many more but Douglass calculated that the true figure should be fifty-two-and-a-half. How he worked this out I don't know. But could Douglass be right? Certainly he had gone to an immense amount of trouble researching Mannock's career.

In the local paper, the Derby Evening Telegraph, there had been a mention of Mick Mannock. Douglass had written in with some information about Mannock and in the letter he stated what he felt was Mannock's score.

He had not said that this was his own calculation but merely stated it as fact. So I replied to the letter pointing out what Mannock's official score was.

These letters sparked off a lively correspondence and a number of letters were sent to me. One of them from the widow of a man who had served as a machine-gunner in the Great War and had been given a fragment of the propeller of Richthofen's Triplane by an Australian machine-gunner. If I would like to collect it I could have it, she wrote.

So I did collect it but over the years it has gone missing!

Douglass had also composed dossiers on many other pilots, getting together more information than anyone else. He had discovered an enormous amount, for example, on the enigmatic South African Beauchamp Proctor, one of the most successful pilots of the war.

During his lifetime Douglass had got together a vast collection of books on World War One aviation including all the rarities. For example, a signed copy of Eddie Rickenbacker's autobiography written in the early 1920s.

I went over to see Douglass one evening in early winter and despite our clash in the local paper he was pleased to see me and made me welcome. Clearly there was much to discuss and, as explained, he was immensely knowledgeable.

The house was badly in need of re-decoration... Douglass had more important things to do than worry about décor and the place was piled with World War One aviation books.

Despite the chilly evening we sat in an unheated room but with so much to talk about we hardly noticed the cold. A box room upstairs was crammed from floor to ceiling with aviation books. He showed me all the dossiers he had compiled on the various fighter aces, all crammed with material new to me.

As well as collecting books he had done his utmost to see as many of the surviving World War One pilots as possible. Among them was 'Mad Major' Chris Draper who had commanded the Royal Naval Air Service Squadron No. 8, the famous Naval 8, when the squadron was at Mont St. Eloi, close to 40 Squadron in 1917/18 though this was after Lionel Blaxland's time. Chris Draper had flown under the Thames bridges as a publicity stunt in the 1950s.

Surprisingly Douglass had never met Lionel Blaxland but after I had told him about my discussions with Lionel he assured me that he would make a point of seeing him. Whether or not he did so I never found out because not long after that he was killed by a fox!
Going home in his car on the A38 near Burnaston Airport a fox darted across the snow covered road. His car hit the fox which jammed the steering. The car went off the road and Douglass was killed.

Shortly afterwards my wife, Edna, was at the hairdressers when she heard the lady in the next chair discussing Douglass' books. She lived next door to his mother and she told Edna that a book dealer had been to see her and had made an offer for the books. Needless to say I raced round to see Mrs Whetton.

The dealer had offered £3,000 but she had not made any decision so I offered her a bit more. I explained that Douglass was a Derbyshire man and that I was a fellow collector who had met him. If the books went to me they would stay in Derbyshire with a fellow aviation enthusiast. She said she would think it over.

The next thing I heard was that the dealer had got the lot. He had been to see her again and told her that if they went to him they would be housed in a magnificent library in a beautiful Cotswold manor house. Collectors would come from all over the world to look at and handle his books. The unmentioned punchline was that they would all be sold!

FURTHER READING

If you have enjoyed the book and would like to read more about those incredible days then here are a few ideas.

The one book you must read is, in my opinion, the best of all the books written by a pilot who flew in the war: *Days of Combat* by Sholto Douglas.

For more on 40 Squadron *An Airman's Wife* by Aimee McHardy, *Fighter Pilot* by McScotch (William MacLanachan), *Winged Warriors* by Barry M. Marsden and *Wings Over the Somme* by Gwilym Lewis.

The aircraft are superbly described in the Harleyford publications: *Fighter Aircraft of the 1914-1918 War* and *Bomber and Reconnaisance Aircraft of the 1914-1918 War*. Another essential Harleyford book is *Richthofen and the 'Flying Circus'*.

For a general view of the Great War I can recommend *Tommy* by Richard Holmes and *The Sword Bearers* by Correlli Barnett.

These books and all the others listed below are from my library and were consulted when writing *Richthofen Jagdstaffel Ahead*. So my thanks to all the authors, past and present.

You do not, however, have to buy any of them as your local library will be pleased to supply them for you at modest cost.

ARTHUR, Max *When This Bloody War is Over* (Piatkus, 2001). The songs were a vital part of the war years and this book lists and gives the words of all the most popular ones. By the same author: *Last Post: The Final Word From Our First World War Soldiers* (Phoenix 2005) The very last survivors give their accounts of the war.

BARNETT, Correlli *The Swordbearers: Supreme Command in the First World War* (Eyre and Spottiswode 1963) The supreme commanders on both sides who held millions of lives in their hands. A marvellous book.

BATCHELOR, John and Cooper, Bryan *Fighter: A History of Fighter Aircraft* (MacDonald 1973) Bryan wrote the text, John painted the illustrations. Both are men of outstanding talent and their work is featured in the book. Bryan also has a further string of books to his credit on factual subjects including World War One plus, for good measure, two novels.

BATCHELOR, John *Encyclopaedia of Flight, History of Flight, Naval Aircraft* plus fourteen other books covering everything from artillery, helicopters, battleships, submarines and handguns! But this is only a fractional part of his talent – as an aviation artist and illustrator he is unsurpassed covering everything from sixteenth century armour to modern aeroplanes. In Purnell's *History of the First World War* and *History of the Second World War* he provided an astonishing 1163 illustrations. It is quite impossible to list the number of books and magazines here to which he has contributed illustrations and, in addition to all that, he has turned his hand to ceramic illustrations and has designed postage stamps for no less than forty-four countries.

BARTLETT, C.P.O. *In the Teeth of the Wind: The Story of a Naval Pilot on the Western Front 1916 1918* (Leo Cooper 1994) Another book of compelling interest written by a pilot who flew in those dangerous skies.

BOWYER, Chaz *Royal Flying Corps Communiques 1917-1918* (Grub Street 1998) Essential information by a distinguished World War One aviation historian.

COLE, Christopher *Royal Flying Corps 1915-1916* (William Kimber 1959) Detailed analysis and by the same author *Royal Flying Corps Communiques 1918* (Tom Donovan Publishing 1990) More vital information.

COOPER, Bryan *The Ironclads of Cambrai* (Cassell 1967) The introduction of the tank in warfare, 1917. Huge advance made but no plans to follow it up.

DOUGLAS, Sholto *Years of Combat* (Collins 1963) In my opinion the best of all books written by a wartime pilot. It really conveys the spirit of the times.

DRAPER, Chris *The Mad Major* (Air Review Ltd 1962) An amazing man! Flew everything during the war years, commanded Camel Squadron Naval 8 and flew under the Thames bridges in the 1950s.

FRANKS, Norman, Guest, Russell and Bailey, Frank W *Bloody April….Black September* (Grub Street 1995) Marvellous stuff! The two most momentous months for allied air losses in the whole of the war by three renowned World War One aviation historians.

FRANKS, Norman, Bailey Frank W. and Duiven, Rick *The Jasta War Chronology* (Grub Street 1998) A complete listing of claims and losses August 1916-November 1918. By the same authors: *The Jasta Pilots* (Grub Street 1992) Painstaking and exhaustive research, not to be missed.

FRANKS, Norman, Guest, Russell and Allegi, Gregory *Above the War Fronts* (Grub Street 1997) A complete record of the British two-seater bomber pilot and observer aces, the British two-seater fighter/observer aces and the Belgian, Italian Austro-Hungarian and Russian Fighter aces 1914-1918. That says it all!

GIBBONS, Floyd *The Red Knight of Germany: Baron Von Richthofen Germany's Great War Airman* (Cassell 1930) The first book on Richthofen, still remarkably readable today.

HAMMERTON, Sir John (Editor) *Aerial Wonders of our Time* (1936?) One of those massive tomes covering everything in aviation right from the earliest days with much about 1914-1918. A book packed with interest.

HOLMES, Richard *Tommy: The British Soldier on the Western Front 1914-1918* (2006) A distinguished historian who produces compelling documentaries on the Great War. A superlative book covering the whole war.

HARLEYFORD PUBLICATIONS, various highly knowledgeable 1914-1918 aviation authors including Norman Franks, Bruce Robertson, Lammerton, Cheeseman, Nowarra and Brown. *Fighter Aircraft of the 1914-1918 War, Reconnaissance and Bomber Aircraft of the 1914-1918 War, Air Aces of the 1914-1918 War, Sopwith the Man and his Aircraft, Fokker the Man and his Aircraft, Von Richthofen and the "Flying Circus"*. I cannot speak too highly of these books which are absolutely packed with information and you can refer to them time and time again. They have been of enormous help in writing my book.

JONES, Ira *King of Airfighters: The Biography of Major Mick Mannock* (Nicholson and Watson 1935) The diminutive Ira Jones was no mean airfighter himself with 40 victories. He flew with Mannock and hero-worshiped him. Ira also served in the RAF in the Second World War. Another must-read book.

JACKSON, Robert *Air War Flanders 1918* (Airlife Publishing 1998) A bit later than Lionel Blaxland's time but essential reading.

KILDUFF, Peter *Richthofen, Beyond the Legend of the Red Baron* (Arms and Armour Press 1993) Know all there is to know about Richthofen? Not until you have read this book!

KIERNAN, R.H. *Captain Albert Ball* (John Hamilton 1933) Impetuous, devil-may-care, shoot 'em-up-regardless Albert Ball was one of the first aces. Another book that demands to be read!

LEWIS, Gwilym *Wings Over the Somme* (1976 but re-published by Bridge Books, Wrexham 1994) Another book by a pilot who flew in 40 Squadron with Mannock but in 1918, after Lionel Blaxland's time. His wartime letters have survived so another valuable insight into those days.

MARSDEN, Barry M. *Winged Warriors: Derbyshire Fighter Pilots in World War One* (Ryestone Publications 2003) A modest but highly informative book by the talented aviation historian. Bill Bond is, of course, featured.

McCUDDEN, James *Flying Fury: The Adventures of England's Great Pilot who Brought Down Fifty Seven German Planes* (John Hamilton 1918) Jimmy McCudden studied the German planes, pilots and tactics and developed air combat into an art. Essential reading.

MORRIS, Joseph *The German Air Raids on Great Britain 1914-1918* (Sampson Low, Marston & Co. Undated but 1920s or 30s) Another heavyweight tome, packed with information.

McHARDY, Aimée *An Airman's Wife: A True Story of Lovers Separated by War* (First published 1918 but re-published by Barry M. Marsden. Grub Street 2005) A touching love story and an insight into flying in 40 Squadron with Blaxland and Mannock, 1917.

McSCOTCH, (William MacLanachan) *Fighter Pilot* (George Routledge and Son Ltd. 1936. Re-published by Cedric Chivers Ltd. 1972) Flew with Blaxland and Mannock in 40 Squadron, 1917. Arguably the most badly designed dust wrapper in the history of aviation literature but don't be put off as the book is a marvellous insight into flying in those days. He was one of the lucky ones who survived!

NORMAN, Aaron *The Great Air War: The Men, the Planes, the Saga of Military Aviation; 1914-1918* (Macmillan, 1968) A massive book written by an American author so with a trans-Atlantic view of the conflict.

RUSSELL, D.A. *The Book of Bristol Aircraft* (The Bristol Aircraft Company 1946) Details of the planes produced by the company including the Bristol Scout and the outstanding Bristol Fighter.

REVELL, Alex *The Vivid Air* (William Kimber 1978) The story of Gerald and Michael Constable Maxwell, descendants of one of the great families from the Scottish Borders. Gerald flew in the First World War, Michael in the Second, also in 56 Squadron. Gerald went to France with 56 Squadron, the first to have the new SE5as. It was to become one of the foremost fighter squadrons of the war and Gerald scored 27 victories. Fellow pilots were among the greatest: Ball, McCudden, Rhys Davids, Hoidge, Lewis, Crowe, Knaggs and Meintjes. In the Second World War Gerald was the station commander at Ford, Sussex. Another must read book!

SMITH, Anthony *Machine-gun: The Story of the Men and the Weapon that Changed the Face of War* Piatkus, 2002) All you could possibly want to know about machine-guns and their development.

TAYLOR, John W.B. *Jane's Fighting Aircraft of World War 1* (Jane's Publishing Co, 1919) A truly massive tome, crammed with interest.

UDET, Ernst *Ace of the Black Cross* (Newnes, undated. 1930's?) Udet was second only to Richthofen in victories scored. He survived the war and helped in the formation of the Luftwaffe but committed suicide in the early days of World War Two. A fascinating look at the air war from the other side of the lines.

WILSON, Sandy *Ivor* (Michael Joseph, 1975). The biography of Ivor Novello. "What the hell is he doing here?" I hear you shout! Patience, I can explain. He was, believe it or not, an RNAS pilot and his songs, over 50 of them written during the war, together with his contribution to the musical theatre were tremendous morale boosters. The most popular song of the War, *Keep the Home Fires Burning* was written by Ivor. Yes, he deserves a place here.

INDEX

Italics denote photographs or illustrations.